FULLY
COMMITTED

The Sacred Sojourn of NOW

Laura JE Hamilton

BALBOA.PRESS
A DIVISION OF HAY HOUSE

Balboa Press books may be ordered through booksellers or by contacting:

Balboa Press
A Division of Hay House
1663 Liberty Drive
Bloomington, IN 47403
www.balboapress.com
844-682-1282

Because of the dynamic nature of the Internet, any web addresses or links contained in this book may have changed since publication and may no longer be valid. The views expressed in this work are solely those of the author and do not necessarily reflect the views of the publisher, and the publisher hereby disclaims any responsibility for them.

The author of this book does not dispense medical advice or prescribe the use of any technique as a form of treatment for physical, emotional, or medical problems without the advice of a physician, either directly or indirectly. The intent of the author is only to offer information of a general nature to help you in your quest for emotional and spiritual well-being. In the event you use any of the information in this book for yourself, which is your constitutional right, the author and the publisher assume no responsibility for your actions.

Any people depicted in stock imagery provided by Getty Images are models, and such images are being used for illustrative purposes only. Certain stock imagery © Getty Images.

Print information available on the last page.

ISBN: 979-8-7652-3023-7 (sc)
ISBN: 979-8-7652-3024-4 (e)

Balboa Press rev. date: 06/21/2022

Contents

Introduction

To Be Or Not To Be

We will return to where we started and know it for the first time.

Every journey begins with a first step in the direction of that which we set our sights on but rarely is it ever a straight path there. And often we'll find there is no path at all because that is exactly what we came to blaze as the way showers of the New Orderly World we are NOW bringing to life together.

Five years ago I set out to write this book, except this book was not even on the radar screen of that version of me's mind. I was still green, as the saying goes, which means I hadn't experienced all the colours changing seasons bring out in the natural world around and within us yet.

There was so much I had no clue about, nor even eyes to see what was there for me before I knew to look for it, yet because I never gave up you now get to see what I gleaned from my own journey to becoming FULLY COMMITTED to being me and now offer as wisdom gained from the sacred sojourn I went through to bring this back to you. My hope is that it will inspire you to push through the dark knights of the ego and dark-light fight of the soul when you too will be tested and tried to see just how committed you are to living fully in the NOW.

I want to start out by thanking everyone I've met along the way, especially those who have loved and supported me and also those who used and abused me. Each of you helped me see the pattern I had of placing my power in the hands of external authority figures I thought could wield it better than I could. What I learned from experience is that energy flows where our attention goes so NOW is the time to refocus on the Divine without the lines that used to define who and whose we thought we needed to be.

This is a controversial tale to tell because it exposes the lies that have been masquerading as truth for longer than we can remember. His-story has been sold as ours and good people have traded their TEEAM of energetic resources: Time, Energy, Effort, Attention, Money for an illusory life that feels empty without loved ones to share it with.

We have been conditioned to compete with others in order to look out for me and mine when the Divine asks us to shift our focus from #metoo to #wetoo for we are all in this together and must remember that the way we know we are suffering is when we see another suffer.

Before the sacred was capitalized on and turned secret for the benefit of the few, at the expense of the many, there was a question asked of those who wished to become law'ds of their lives by learning how to use the universal laws that direct life in this material reality. That question was "How do you know when you are suffering?"

In order to gain access to the sacred in-sights wise students of life had gleaned from their journey and gave freely to those with eyes to see and ears to hear truth in all of its simplicity one had to demonstrate compassion for life, lest their demons cause strife in the communities they came from and would return to when they were through.

The truth has been hidden beneath lies designed to control and confine anyone willing to submit to an outer authority to write the script of the life we came here to lead as originals.

Most have heard the line "To be, or not to be: that is the question" from the Shakespearean play *Hamlet* where the main character contemplates the purpose of life and suicide while speaking his thoughts aloud despite being alone on the stage (called a soliloquy). What we have failed to see is that we are each being called to answer that question by lawfully claiming the right to lead our lives as we see fit (self-govern) despite the fight that comes with reclaiming our power from corp-orations that need our TEEAM to feed the machine.

In the Shakespearean play *As You Like It* he reveals more truth but mixes in an agenda that begins to erode our belief in our ability to choose the roles we will play in the life we lead: All the world's a stage,

And all the men and women merely players;
They have their exits and their entrances,
And one man in his time plays many parts (Jaques,
Act 2 Scene 7)

This part is true and you are called to fill in the rest your own way by righting the wrongs present-lie said to be best, lest your soul be made less whole because you sold your cells to an-other before seeing how that tied you to a ship mast (flagpole) that is going under.

Pirates will plunder (steal goods from a place or person, typically using force) for that is what they do best and in order to recruit you they will make you feel less. This is where our fears and insecurities are preyed on by energetic entities we were taught to revere yet many have failed to see how the light and dark gather legions that take our TEEAM whether that be in the name of freedom, spirituality, politics, business or religion. Our energy is what entities need to feed off of and the longer we stay focused on 'us vs them' the longer we miss the point that we are all in this together.

We have been duped and must see the truth behind Plato's "Allegory of the Cave."

An allegory is a story, poem, or picture that can be interpreted to reveal a hidden meaning, typically a moral or political one. The gist of the cave allegory is that a group of people live chained to the wall of a cave all their lives facing a blank wall with shadow projections from the fire behind them. The people give names and meaning to the shadows and believe them to be part of their "prisoner's reality" even though they were not accurate representations of the real world.

Plato's allegory portrays a philosopher, or 'woke' one, who has freed themselves from their chains and managed to step outside the cave to see what the shadows really are.

When we return to share our findings with those who have never left the cave, our stories sound 'too out there,' far-fetched and unbelievable to those still oblivious to the lies they don't want to think they've been deceived by. Cognitive dissonance is an internal battle between the known/familiar and unknown/unfamiliar that brings up uncomfortable emotions we don't know how to process because we've been living in an emotionally repressed society we were led to believe we were free within, but only to a point.

I crossed that line when I 'woke up' and got myself locked up under the Mental Health Act which exposed the current-lie corrupted system in a way I hadn't expected and may not have believed had I not experienced it firsthand. It was a traumatic experience and I traumatized many of those closest to me by going through it very publicly. I scorched a lot of Earth around me by letting my scared side run the show and I got to reach some very low points emotionally for having done so.

After two and a half years obsessing about 'the book' that took so much of my TEEAM, I followed my inner guidance to make a crazy call to do what this book is meant to do now but my plan and the Divine's plan had a different timeline and that version of me couldn't write this story until I lived it. It took another two and a half years afterwards, with the help of a Pendemic that was designed to divide and conquer from the inside out, for me to break free of the entities wearing different uni-forms to see how much more power-full 'being free' is to 'having free-dom' in a domain as controlled by FEAR as we've been living our lives up till now in.

People come into our lives for a reason, season or lifetime and our Belief Systems (BS) will be used to keep us feeling safely separate from one another until we bring the sacred back into our cult-u-rally accepted way of life, for whole-i-stick (holistic) practices are a true-lie holy way of life.

My Mom's favourite Berenstain Bears book is *The Bike Lesson* and whenever things don't go to plan she quotes its moral: "Now that is what you should not do, so let that be a lesson to you." And after all I've been through and brought others into in the process I have learned many lessons the hard way and hope to offer insights I believe may save you the shame, pain and drama I went through to bring them to you now. I hope to repair some of the damage done in the process but forgiveness is an INNER job that helps us show up whole and be where we are when we're there with the ones we call friends in the end.

Don't accept any of what's to come as truth or go-spell unless it resonates which is what you must do with all the BS you will come to and work through in a world that wishes to feed off of you and your power to choose; we will either choose intentionally or unintentionally and entities love the unconscious and compliant most. Use the power of discernment to decide for yourself what all of this means to and for you, and what you're going to do with it for that is how information becomes useful.

Discernment: the ability to judge well.

Remember too that our energy is like a well that is either being taken from or added to and factor that into your practice of discernment, asking yourself whether something will leave you feeling better for having inter-acted with it or whether it drains you and your energy. That's not a common consideration where discernment is concerned but I propose it's one that could serve you well if you're willing to notice how your feelings show up as sign posts that will direct you toward your highest good and the greater good as a result.

Let us dig into what it means to be a PEACEFULL INNER Warrior United and Untied from the outdated Ma-trix that puts the creator of all into boxes (words) of BS (Belief Systems) that make us think we believe differently when it's all the same in different packaging; like the pirate ships that carry a box of flags they change the banner of when people stop trusting one, learn to recognize when an entity is trying to overtake the energy den (E-den) of you.

We are all on the same mothership (Ma Terre=Earth) and we are responsible for her and the life she supports so let us dare to do better at caring for it all, our cells included.

Resentment will not help your boat float any better, it will only weaken you over time as it did me while I unpacked all that went into becoming the one who brought this to you now. We are meant to walk one another home to our own heart centre as the 'great ones' of the past did while they lived. Now it is our turn to not only follow their example but to be an example for those looking to us now as the current players on the field of life.

The Story of Not Enough, Victims & The Flip Side

If I said I've restarted this book hundreds of times over the years, it wouldn't be an underestimate. And I even finished three manuscripts I deemed 'not enough' because I trusted the wrong people to care for and critique my creative babies before I had the courage to trust in my own enoughness.

The story of 'not enough' is practically universal and empathic ones, like myself, often have an even harder time because we fail to discern what is ours and what is perceived in our environment or is being projected onto us, as if it is ours.

Empathy: the ability to understand and share the feelings of another.

The story of 'not enough' plagues us all because hurting people hurt people and before the age of seven we lack a conscious mind to filter out the input we receive from our environment. It just all goes directly into the subconscious mind which acts as an internal filing cabinet for all of the Belief Systems (BS) we will run our lives based on until we decide to govern our minds responsibly without judgement of what is currently there.

It is the reason Greek philosopher Aristotle famously said, "Give me a child until he is 7 and I will show you the man."

That may be true for many who do not dare to question the BS governing their lives but the fact you are reading this now suggests you are willing to take charge of your INNER world so you can create an outer REALITY you enjoy living. Please know this will challenge existing beliefs and disturb those around you who are used to you thinking, acting and believing a certain way. This is what is most familiar and convenient to those who know you to be as you've always been.

Cognitive dissonance is the result of two competing ideas co-existing in the same space, and when you start to bring about change (even for the better) it will create discomfort because you will no longer think, act or believe the way you did before; that also means those around you (and within you) will have to adapt to the new you and many are content with the status quo. You will just have to say "no, I choose to consciously change myself and my cells because expansion is what I came here to experience" and even if you may not know the way yet, by the time you are through the transformation process you will have experience to share with others who care to hear your tales which they may learn from too.

Believe it and trust me to show you the way, as I have went through the transformation process with varying levels of consciousness so many times I have learned tips and insights that I know can offer you keys for your process too. And please also know that part of the reason this took me so long to complete is because I struggled through each transformation of my self-image until I agreed to step fully into the i-mage role of my own creative power.

Mage: the ability to attain objectives or acquire knowledge or wisdom using supernatural means.

Supernatural: attributed to some force beyond scientific understanding or the laws of nature.

Law of nature: a regularly occurring or apparently inevitable phenomenon observable in human society. The fundamentals are called the '7 Natural Laws' which are: Attraction, Polarity, Rhythm, Relativity, Cause and Effect, Gender/Gestation and Perpetual Transmutation of Energy *(I will inadvertently cover these in this book but you may wish to re-search them further given their applicability to the creative process)*.

For a long time I turned to others to comfort and guide me without seeing how I was losing personal power in the process of doing so. Karpman's drama triangle depicts this dysfunctional power dynamic well and features the victim, rescuer and persecutor/ punisher archetypes. We commonly play out these parts with others and also within ourselves.

An archetype is a familiar pattern that can be recognized by a word. Karpman's three work together to keep the victim disempowered by a punisher who keeps them looking for a rescuer to save them from a problem they feel incapable of solving on their own; Disney popularized this dynamic with storylines revolving around a helpless princess, evil villain (often a stepmother) and a dashing prince who saves the day but it doesn't have to be that way.

The flip side is The Empowerment Dynamic (TED) where the victim becomes the creator, the rescuer becomes the challenger and the persecutor becomes the coach who supports and facilitates clarity by asking questions that help the creator turn inward to find answers they hadn't previously been aware of, hence feeling like a victim.

Coaches often use Neruro-Linguistic Programming (NLP) to help people change the stories they tell themselves and one of the presuppositions of both modalities is that there are no unresourceful people, only unresourceful states.

This shift in perspective helps to separate the person from the behaviour, but what we're going to get into soon is the need to separate the man or woman from the false identity of a person (or any other status that converts our substance into a form that can be owned and directed by a creator outside of the creative source that created us all).

Before we get there however I want to share a powerful story of a gardener who found a struggling butterfly trying to break free of its cocoon the way we are all doing with the illusions we have taken on as false skin, like the wolf who wears the sheep's clothing.

A gardener was tending to his garden, for which he was a guard in, when he noticed a cocoon. Soon it began to vibrate and wiggle as the one within tried to free itself of its shell. The gardener pulled up a chair to watch the miraculous emergence of that which had not yet been revealed to the world. The butterfly within efforted for hours and the man got bored with waiting so 'helped' the butterfly by cutting a small hole the former caterpillar was able to pull itself out of. When it did the man thought it was the strangest looking butterfly he'd ever seen, with a swollen body and small wings that did not seem big enough to support it.

The gardener carried on about his work in hopes he'd get to see the butterfly's first flight except it didn't seem able to move far beyond the spot where it had emerged. For what the man didn't know was that the struggle is required for the butterfly to redistribute the fluids from its body into its wings so, in effect, by trying to save the butterfly (and himself) time and effort the man actually sealed its fate to never fly and die on the spot where it emerged. This is directly tied to the law of gender/gestation that says everything goes through a natural unfoldment process that is unique to that being. Trying to rush the process often causes more harm than help despite good intentions so learning to hold a sacred space for another's unfoldment is truly the greatest gift we can give one another; this is presence.

A victim will remain disempowered if they believe they need to be rescued by someone or something outside of themselves. For generally we only find a way when we have no other choice, like the butterfly would have done if it had been given the time and space to unfold naturally. Dare to care enough to let another share their tales without trying to solve their problems for them; sometimes we just need a witness in order to reintegrate insecure parts of ourselves we've called back after years of neglect and rejection and aren't fully comfortable with yet. Holding space for another's unfoldment is a gift that does not require words.

It requires non-judgemental presence and compassionate connection that accepts the process of unfoldment which is often messy and unpredictable but worth the wait in the end. It is a gift we can best give others when we've experienced it and learned to give it to ourselves.

While it is true that hurting people hurt people, it is also true that healed people heal people so dare to do the INNER work and you will be able to be of great service to the world!

Better To Be In Charge Of Your Energy Than In Control

2

We are living in an insane www.urld where the truth seems stranger than fiction, for much of what we have come to believe is based on a legal fiction that we have all been sold into by the BS we thought was in our best interest to believe.

I believe it is time for us to wake up from the Matrix like Neo did in the documentary-style movie that was not sold as such. For that is how black magic works; evil must be invited in and the rules must be written for prospective victims to see or hear before their 'fate' is sealed and presence to heal or feel truth is lost.

To some this will seem too unbelievable to accept and if that is you I would encourage you to consider how shutting down the source of alternative information in this instance relates to how you do the same in other areas of your life too. For how we do anything is how we do everything because that is the way patterns work.

Neuroplasticity is a scientific interpretation of the mental patterns we ingrain within our minds and then use to create our future, based on the choices we make now. We'll get into that deeper later but for now I'd like to simply offer a significant distinction early on.

Aim to be *in charge* of your life instead of trying to be *in control.*

Control is a dysfunctional creative energy that tries to compartmentalize things, including people, for the benefit of the one calling the shots. It requires the contraction of one for the sake of another and it is what modern societies have been based on, especially during the attempted corporatocratic takeover that is current-lie underway.

Being in charge is about taking command of the energy in and around us for the sake of directing it in a way that will serve us better than a contracted and controlled state of being ever could. We've just been taught the opposite of truth in this inverted and perverted reality so when truth is felt we think we must have it wrong, because the history books and mainstream media say otherwise; how convenient for the creators of his-story who require we deny our power-full nature in exchange for the stories we're told are true and 'historical' or 'scientific'.

It is time for us to recognize we are spiritual beings having a human experience and as energetic beings at our core we feel truth when we are able to call our power back to the pre-sent moment, just as many of the celebrated ones did during their lives. I'll add that what many of these great men and women stood for was changed when stories were written about them, for the benefit of the one commissioning the storyteller.

I believe it is time for us to shift our focus away from his-story so that we can write our own in a sustainable way that prioritizes people (life) over profits.

We must begin to see the power of the worlds we create with the words we use, and the deeper (often hidden) meanings behind associations not readily apparent at first glance.

The word profit is a prime example for how oblivious we are of what becomes obvious once the lies are exposed. Ob(lie)vious to obvious, you see?

Profits are how corp-orations have become the prophets of our time because hidden hands pull the strings of the men and women working on be-half of it who then change the rules of the game, within their corporation, that consumers must abide by. And so it is that creators are converted into consumers who buy things to become something more than they feel they are without the thing.

Consumers feed off of what exists. Creators find ways to improve what exists or bring something new entirely into existence.

Profits come from creations owned or made by corporations.

Prophets see what has not yet come to pass and bring it into REALITY by taking inspired actions that feel right even if it may not seem reasonable or be respected at the time.

I wouldn't call myself a prophet and yet I remember running upstairs from the basement at my Grandparents' where I've lived for most of the five years it took to finally write this man-u-script of the book I say rewrote me before the world got to see it. I remember excitedly telling my Grandma that I'd realized I was getting the equivalent of a phD from life school and 'the book' would be the equivalent of my thesis paper.

I also told her I was essentially creating a new religion that was 'no re-legion' which was befitting given I'd been saved from religious indoctrination by their influence, much to my Mother's dismay. For that I am sorry but not sorry because I believe I am here to do what the man coined 'Jesus' did and more, as he said we would and could, and I don't believe I'm special in that claim. I just maybe gathered the courage to say it before I was named as one who could and it became a popularized concept as it was intended to be when 'the man' seeded it into our collective consciousness, before its meaning was misconstrued.

Doing so has not, admittedly, been easy yet if not me then who will do that which I see the need to do NOW? And the same goes for you with that which you are called to do.

I have no control over how this message is received, nor the backlash I get from putting such a controversial and empowering message out there, but I am in charge of making it happen. And I wish to remind you that I am but a mirror for you to see through, as 'He' was too.

What if "I am the way" actually referred to the power words that "I am" are as a creative force we create sentences from that we live out based on our beliefs about what comes next?

What if the intended meaning of "I am the way" was to say "I am" is the way we start creating better worlds (realities) with the words we choose to complete our sentences with, to either serve us or work against us?

Laura JE Hamilton

What if we dared to consider the life sentence we live is based on the sacred words we use to build ourselves and our lives with, lest they become the swords that cut us down and keep us feeling small and control-able in a reality we believe to be 'out of our hands'?

What if we chose to take up our pens and stop signing our lives away to external authorities we've been trained to tie our identities to which empowers them at our expense?

What if we took back our power by becoming more intentional about the words we choose in the sentences we construct our lives with and are willing to accept by external authorities who require our energy to move it forward?

Imagine if we each decided to own our power to create a REALITY (Realistic Evidence Appearing Legit In Tomorrow's Yesterday) that we actually enjoy living and can be proud to account for when our soul returns to the same source we all came from in order to be the change we seek in this world. What a world that might be if we will it to be as we wish!

Power Pits, Parapets & The Story Of Maybe

3

There has never been a time in history that was safe to be empowered for how it makes those who are stand out when everyone else is bowing down to something outside of themselves and their cells.

Prisoners in prison cells are converted into a status that grant external authority figures power over their lives in an obvious way yet until we see the corrupted nature of the REALITY we've all been living in, we will remain prisoners to a fiction that dis-empowers for the benefit of an-other (entity) who passes the buck onto those men and women acting on its be-half.

Corporations have compartmentalized our way of thinking so we don't see the bigger picture and the response-ability we each have for the choices we make but that was part of the devil's plan to gain souls. And before you think I'm talking about a little red creature with horns and a tail, recognize that the devil is spelt 'lived backwards', plain and simple.

The real e-state being fought for in this battle for souls is our mental space because that is how we discern or filter information and decide which formation or legion we will join forces with. And while accounting for devious or evil (live backwards) choices is never i-deal or comfortable, doing so a-head of the end of your time here will give your soul time to heal into more wholeness before you depart and are forced to restart your next life with fewer soul fragments than you could have if you started now for the benefit of us all.

Like the popular Chinese proverb says "The best time to plant a tree was twenty years ago. The second best time to plant a tree is now" so let us begin to dis-cover the power within so that we can stand on the solid ground of truth to-gather without submitting to external authority that only holds power because we have given it ours without making the connection.

The original President of the John Maxwell Team was Paul Martinelli who greatly impacted my path and to whom I have much gratitude. As a student and teacher of the Universal Laws in relation to being an entrepreneur, he often taught that we create by default or design; it wasn't until I fully committed to becoming an i-mage of my own self-image that I saw how many programs were running in my unconscious by default despite my efforts to create by design.

This is where my farming heritage came in from a mental perspective and I saw the need to weed the garden of my mind, though doing so was harder done than said.

While living in England with one of Paul's 'hired guns' as my ex used to call himself, I remember him mentioning 'parapets' and misinterpreted him to have said 'power pits' which contextually made sense to me.

As a younge Canadian without castles as a mainstay in my country I didn't realize parapets are the high and low edges along a castle, kingdom or drawbridge that could be hid behind for protection. Subsequently I envisioned a pit full of people vying for power who would try to pull any who rose above the rest back down, like crabs in a bucket; if you want to catch a crab all you need to do is put one in the trap and it will prevent any others from leaving.

The context of the conversation was in reference to David Beckham's rise to success before his metaphoric 'public beheading' when he was blamed for his team's defeat. I was told that, culturally, the English love elevating their own to a point, but after that they love seeing the one who rose and grew 'too big for their britches' come toppling down. If you look into the hidden meaning of the nursery rhyme "Jack and Jill" you'll find reference to the downfall of a King and his Queen, but that's besides the point.

I remember when I first moved to England, for that relationship, and scheduled my first women's empowerment workshop in

Worcester. We hit the streets to hand out flyers one Saturday with minimal success but I was grateful for his willingness to help. I remember his disgust at one woman who had refused the flyer while smoking a cigarette, saying she was already empowered and didn't need it, which maybe from her perspective she was. From his, her actions exposed an incongruence deep within that was driving her toward an early death which did not seem empowered at all and his ego had let her know it.

In Napoleon Hill's book *"Outwitting the Devil"* cigarettes are said to "break down the power of persistence; they destroy the power of endurance; they destroy the ability to concentrate; they deaden and undermine the imaginative faculty, and help in other ways to keep people from using their minds effectively." This work by Napoleon came into my awareness after finishing this manuscript as an audioprogram on YouTube which I recommend with the caveat that everything is filtered through the impure filter of the one writing it and those influencing them; the devil in this dialogue requires the same 'title of respect' used within the legal fiction (his Majesty) which is a relevant parallel we'll get into deeper soon. Where accolades are made to benefits of the industrial revolution and the Rockefeller's contribution to the 'health care system' bear in mind that Andrew Carnegie (industrialist) was a significant sponsor of Napoleon's work; with those biases in mind, listen with all three eyes wide open (referring to the third eye of intuition).

What the Pendemic made clear nearly a century after the exchange that brought in reference to one of the early influencers in the thought leader movement (Napoleon Hill) is that the Western cult-u-re in both countries I've called home have a default directive toward the status quo. Status being a position or rank in relation to others and 'quo' being something received or given for something else, namely the right to stand as equals.

After getting locked up under the Mental Health Act for nearly three weeks in 2019, which served as a significant turning point in my life, I learned that those who create by design instead of default can be seen as a threat to the SYSTEM designed to 'Save Yourself Significant

Time Energy Money' because it challenges the default setting that is geared toward death.

There was a tremendous amount of magick present in the week leading up to that fateful day when I called 9-1-1 to report the system was corrupt and the POLICE were in on it. In retrospect, it was a crazy call to make and I wouldn't do it again as the truth I shared in my 'messy awakening' is more apparent than ever, yet I'm grateful to my soul for going through it without losing my heart for people over profits as was the story that had become so clear to me at that time. I did harden my heart in some ways and have been working on bringing those walls back down in the years since but I am not perfect nor do I claim to be; perfectly imperfect is good enough for me and softening after hardship is a process support helps to get through.

I am especially grateful because of the timing of it all because were it not for that experience there is no way I would have stood my ground the way I have through this attempted corporatocratic takeover that is stealing souls right, left and centre. I also wouldn't have necessarily believed the horror stories that I heard and experienced the energetic patterns of firsthand while in the belly of the beast had I not lived it.

My apparently wreckless behaviour was the result of trying to make something happen, after many attempts to get this book done which became much more than just a book. Writing it became part of my identity and not managing to give myself the gift of accepting the three manuscripts I'd completed prior to then had emotionally scarred me and then I had to work through the trauma of all that call led me to which took a lot of TEEAM.

One story of significance I'd wanted to include I remember telling the police officer who 'formed' me and sent me on a journey I never thought I would take.

It's the story of a farmer who had a herd of mares he would let run free by day and who always returned to the barn at night for shelter, except one day they came back with the most magnificent stallion imaginable who the farmer then had possession of. It was big news in the village so the locals all came to see the stallion the next day and congratulate the farmer for his profitable acquisition.

They congratulated him for being so 'lucky' and the farmer simply shrugged his shoulders and said 'maybe'.

Well the farmer's son was a renowned horse trainer who was known to tame even the wildest stallions so when that magnificent beast bucked him off a few days into training, shattering his leg in several places, all the townspeople came back to share their regrets and confusion at this turn of events and the 'bad luck' it seemed to be. The farmer once again shrugged and said 'maybe?'.

But wouldn't you know there was a war going on in that country that just hadn't reached their village yet so when soldiers came days later, to round up all the able-bodied men and boys, the farmer's son wasn't able to go. The locals came back, having lost their own sons to the campaign, congratulating the farmer who they now said was lucky after all. And as you likely guessed, the farmer responded with 'maybe'.

I remember telling that story to my Mom and her husband when they came to visit me on the second day in the science experiment that is 10th floor St. Joseph's Hospital (Hamilton) which was where I experienced the energetic overlay of the Stanford Prison experiment when they wheeled me in; I hadn't realized the sinister strategy behind that small act of 'demon-strating' I couldn't walk on my own two feet so was made an involuntary ward of a system designed to convert men and women into patients, addicts and dependents (prisoners).

Ward: a person under the care and control of a guardian appointed by their parents or a court (Side note: Hiring legal re-presentation makes one a 'ward of the court' that can be spoke for).

Having lost control of my life at that time, as wards no longer have the final say in what comes their way, I learned being on the other side of an order is not in my (or your) best interest given the ones following orders are not attached to the outcome in the same way we are with what happens to us. And while it took time to make sense of it all, I do believe that going through what I did was a gift to which the farmer would say 'May-be?'.

The Stanford Prison Experiment & My 10ᵗʰ Floor Nightmare

The Stanford Prison experiment took place in the summer of 1971 where male volunteers were offered $15 per day to participate in a study of prison life where some were given guard uniforms to de-individuate them and others were assigned the role of prisoner. It was designed to examine stereotypical conformity and obedience to authority figures, similar to the *Milgram experiment,* and was intended to be a two-week experiment but it had to be terminated early due to the cruelty of some power-tripping guards toward 'prisoners' who knew they were innocent and should never have volunteered for such an experiment. Ironically, at the time I got locked up I was in the interview process to be a 'Corrections Officer' so the scenario was very realistic to me.

I experienced the "professionals" in that unit intentionally avoiding eye contact with patients desperate for connection with someone who cared, phones were taken away upon admission which limited who could even make a call given the pre-programmed nature of today's world and calls were only permitted once every two hours, except during night hours; I knew three numbers by heart and tried everything I could think of in the 24 hours I was held in that horrible place to convince my Dad, Mom and Grandparents to help me get out but they felt I'd went too far and the 'professionals' said I needed to be in there. Such is the way 'woke ones' get played by a system that need us to stay comfortably numb to the toxicity of a death cult(ure) we're now called to help make life affirming once again.

Because I was writing in my journal for much of the night, I know I heard a nurse lie to another patient about the time saying they'd slept for hours and it was the middle of the afternoon when I wasn't allowed to make a call at that time because it was actually the middle of the night. I didn't speak up in that moment because I realized just how precarious my own situation was but because of how I was playing 'the game' there I saw the shame in some (professionals) who hadn't been fully corrupted yet and knew I didn't need to be in there, like the Doctor in the first place who had told me to give him my phone and look up Stanislav Grof's work because he saw my experience for what it was, even though he didn't forewarn me as to what I was about to go through; and then there were others who only saw me as a nuisance who needed medication to settle down when what I really needed was the compassionate care of one willing to be present with unfamiliarity without pre-scripting medications that only polluted my system. But what could they say when the reality is I was speaking an inconvenient truth not commonly accepted but no less true for it?

There were many other elements of that experience that diminished what respect, faith or trust I had in the medical system before then but I got to experience the very real potential of getting lost in a medicated world that would have clouded my clarity of mind, body, heart and soul had I not managed to get myself out when I did.

Because I had travelled a lot and incorporated a company of my own before that time I knew the importance of having correct details on forms so caught the mistake on the first form I was issued which listed my Grandparents' address when my government ID was still registered next door; so it was that I contested the first offer without realizing that was what I was doing.

When they 'corrected' their 'error' and issued me a second offer to con-form to, without my middle names that time, I contested it yet again and was told "it won't matter where you're going" by one of the female officers who did not care about nor for me one bit further than her duty-bound care necessitated. And that was when I legitimately began to fear for my life.

Even though I was still supposedly on a 'voluntary' form at that time, I was not allowed to call a lawyer without getting a physician's permission first, who conveniently was not on duty before they transferred me to the next place; the Mood Disorders Program in Hamilton's Number One Waterfall as I jokingly referred to it which was where I got held 'involuntarily' for more than two weeks after that without ever seeing the form I was being held under. While I finally agreed to take a minimal dose of anti-psychotic medications the man acting as a psychiatrist pre-scribed me, after I realized they wouldn't let me out if I didn't show willingness to comply, I got to experience a mild form of the retrainment programming groups like the Uyghurs and Falun Gong people in China are currently facing which the world must look at now.

It has become clear to all who see the loss of rights and freedoms occurring around the globe that we have become an enslaved people to the BS rules of the ones whose governance we have consented to. And what I experienced firsthand is that the Mental Health Act has become the modern-day witch hunt, normalized and legalized to make sure alternative ones like me don't have a chance to remind the masses of what could be if we take a stand for what can and will be because we choose life instead of following a death cult any longer than we already have.

The WEB We Weave If We Believe In Evil: Event 201

5

From my own experience of transforming my self-image to complete this work, in all the unexpected ways I did, I believe our starting point must be in the acknowledgement of self-worth, self-esteem and self-belief as the WEB we weave our lives with and get caught up in until we believe in our own potential.

As you can imagine, that experience took a toll on my WEB because it changed how I saw myself, how others saw me, and the trauma built up walls within me that took Time, Effort, Energy, Attention and Money to recover from. It also revealed how dysfunctional my INNER world had become as I had not surrendered myself quietly and had in fact made it quite the public performance.

At the time, what I knew to be true but hadn't understood the significance of then, was that my online world had become more important to me than my real one. And in retrospect I see that I simply experienced what the con video game drama made a REALITY for the majority when virtual became the only allegedly 'safe' option to connect through. You see, I refer to COVID-19 as the Certificate Of Vex ID-AI (1+9 are the first and ninth letter of the alpha-bet) or the 'con video game' that made the world con-form in order to stay relevant and after experiencing the loss of my rights and freedoms then, I no longer automatically give 'authority figures' the same level of respect a title, position or status suggests is deserved by default.

Vex: make (someone) feel annoyed, frustrated, or worried, especially with trivial matters.

An interesting added layer to my experience was the fact I had been teaching English to children in China up to the morning of when I made that fateful call, for a company said to have been connected with Kobe Bryant's 'Black Mamba' persona. But that's a tale I heard pieced together afterward by Bishop Larry Gaiters that helped me see how energetically perceptive I had been when feeling I was being observed by more than my students and their parents.

Two additional elements that contributed to the insanity of the call I made revolved around the fact my students and their parents were already dealing with the psychological hardships of lockdowns under the rule of a tyrannical dictatorship, for what else can the Chinese Communist Party (CCP) be considered? I have also heard that Wuhan was the first to go live with 5G technology and the people 'dropping like flies' were experiencing a 'shorting' of their nervous systems. As energetic beings this makes perfect sense and is why I believe the current agendas are all geared toward moving the masses into city centres where the 5G technology has been covertly placed under the cover of a Pendemic that was written.

I believe it's significant to mention that *Event 201* took place in New York City three days after I was able to get myself out of the hospital, which I left the day after I discovered I was 'in red on the board' which meant they couldn't hold me any longer. The fact the man acting as a Psychiatrist personally guaranteed me that I would fail to self-regulate as I informed him I would be doing is shocking and yet those indoctrinated souls who have conformed to the standards of a corrupt system believed there must have been something significantly wrong with me. Yet in the words of Krishnamurti "it is no measure of health to be well adjusted to a profoundly sick society."

As I returned to the basement of my Grandparent's home, with much scorched Earth to repair with them and many others too, I had no idea that representatives for many of the big corporations were meeting for a full day of simulation training to prepare and organize themselves in the event there were to be a Pandemic... if you doubt my words look up 'Event 201 – John Hopkins Center for

Health Security' and see how we have been played by the very ones who have proclaimed themselves to be saviours from a virus that has never been isolated.

It is a tangled web we've weaved indeed and the fight between FEAR and faith is more real than we'd like to believe. Yet what had become clear to me, in my heightened state of awareness at the time I made that fateful call, is how the 'grey ones' or those who try to stay neutral are preyed upon most. And that is when we see how the grey matter in our own brains is the territory being bought and paid for by corporate agendas sold by the men and women working on its behalf.

If you don't know what you stand for you risk falling for just about anything that appeals to the physical senses which is why so many potential creators have been converted into consumers who bow to the power of materialism and commercialism. And then we begin to see why we've been culturally encouraged to avoid controversial topics like religion or politics while socializing in order to not 'ruffle any feathers' or push anyone's buttons unnecessarily.

Yet it is necessary to get back to the virtues that were meant to be at the foundation of both even though commercialism (emphasis on the maximizing of profit at the expense of quality) has perverted their very nature, as we'll dig into deeper soon.

Cults, Ceremonies & The BBQ Business

6

The advent of the internet has led to the greatest disconnection between one another and the source of creation but it's easy to miss without eyes to see the lies corporations have sold in the name of evolving consciousness and interconnection.

What I now see is that I was living a pre-con vid experience before everyone else was forced into a REALITY I'd chose after leaving my life in England when I started selling the program so much of my identity had become tied to in the seven years I was actively involved with the John Maxwell Team (JMT) as a Founding Partner, Faculty girlfriend, Coaching Partnerships Coordinator, Program Coordinator and event support at ten Certification events after my own. I'd had such a unique vantage point from all these experiences within that corporation that my affiliation with and membership to it meant more to me than familial relationships with people who've never understood my alternative ways and believed me to be part of a cult but did their best to love me anyway; there is truth to their point of view, but not in the way we've commonly thought.

A cult is "a system of religious veneration and devotion directed toward a particular figure or object" which is the foundation of the 'cult you are' (culture) part of. And so because the JMT had a culture of servant leadership at its core it can be said that I was part of a cult that helped me think outside of the box of 'me and mine' in the name of being of service to the greater good. When I went through my awakening experience shortly after writing the story that will follow though, this BS was fighting within me because in trying to serve the world without a position, status or appointment to warrant the influence I was trying to make, I was neglecting my own life and loved ones in a dysfunctional way I hadn't fully owned.

Had it not been for the relationship I was in for the first four years of my involvement with the JMT, I likely would have been more influenced by the religious perspectives John brought to the program as a Pastor of 30 years before he'd 'put the cookies on the lowest shelf' by translating biblical texts for the secular world and corporate environment. To my ex I am incredibly grateful for that because unbinding ourselves from cultural dog-ma is difficult, for what does a dog do when it is backed into a corner? The bitch (female dog) bites and funny enough that was very much part of my story at the time I 'woke up' from the Matrix and saw how devious Ma's tricks can be when the woman feels threatened, as I'd wrote on the plane ride back from Arizona to DC the day before life as I knew it irrevocably changed forever after.

That whole trip, from my days at the Hilton Embassy Suites to the flight back and overnight stay with a boyfriend I'd betrayed while away, was other-worldly to say the least and part of why I felt more significant than my Earthly results to that point suggested was true. But nonetheless I made it through without losing myself, my connection to spirit or my heart in the process; I credit my faith and Divine grace for that, without having put the creator in a box.

For more than two years I have sat with the story I wrote as I flew into DC to layover without knowing how to share it or even when to do so, as the experience that followed disturbed me on every level and took time to recover from. I also wanted to be wrong as certain loved ones told me I was, yet I believe that now it is time to share a perspective meant to help us steer clear from the dangerous waters we've been sailing in unawares:

The BBQ Business – We Fry The Evil: How
The Old World Had To Fry & Why

The Reptilians took office by stealing from the people and preying on their own innocence which is why we've needed to put God in a box. To keep ourselves feeling safe.

The old order needed to be right and needed the warriors to forget that we are all potential wolves in sheep's clothing (*not meant to be a reference to the Fabian Society*).

What we had forgot was that we are all wolves, because that is what magick people are, except when we are trapped by fear and our own reptilian nature kicks in to try to keep us all safe. Safely separate has been all that was needed because the women were willing to let the men lead and counsel from behind as all great leaders do; except who in the kingdom within is sitting on the throne? For our SCARED or SACRED sides lead very different lives.

And so it is in this life that we must seek to partner with someone worthy and noble of our attention.

Our intention is what must pave the way and the people will say "who are you to be brave? Power-full? Gorgeous? Or Fabulous?" as *Our Deepest Fear* says.

The evil will pit the true against those who wish to study the pure hearted because they want in on the secret that only the most powerful have known.

The secret is that there is a battle between good and evil taking place now and it's happening on every level that counts.

The Knights who are true are called to step into their role as Kings of their own courts and to stop trying to give their power to people who are intoxicated by their own egos.

When the pure hearted awaken we can be fearful of how others judge because they are not ready and can't really handle their own power and so they place theirs in the hands of others and veil the unrest in the most fun and reasonable way possible.

Our inner child is the gate keeper to growing up and we must find someone who is as true as Dr. Drew. He came here to keep her safe and his Queen knows that crazy is not good for children because it's just "too much."

And so to protect her children she will close her heart and make her creative babies her everything. And he, the King, will become the one she taunts, just to take back the power she has so freely given because she is true and noble too.

She will become like the snake and scorpion who lurch out in the darkness of ignorance, at the ones standing in their light, because it is too bright and it is confusing her children.

She, the Mother, just wants to keep her babies safe but she forgot that none of us ever make it safely out of life alive.

Every dawn has its setting sun and every evening precedes a new day of hope, with people of heart as the leaders or as the spoiled brats who must try to take all the power.

Even those who are pure will fall into the trap sometimes because what we must remember is what the Old Cherokee grandfather told his grand-one. He told his grand-baby the tale of two wolves fighting within him who represent the forces of God and the force of the wounded dog.

The fear-full will pounce on the moments of vulnerability that the true ones expose by showing all their cards too fast (as I was soon to do).

The chariot drivers we choose are thus incredibly important because when the snake shows up at your door as a beautiful distraction, the Queen must trust herself enough to see what's really happening before it's too late.

She must ask herself what must be let go of to learn to see the darkness for what it is.

There is so much pain in this world that we are trying to kill the Mother.

The Captains of the night skies (I wrote while I was flying) are as important as the ones at sea and everything in between because they realize they are just ants too.

We are all just ants playing out our parts at the right time and it is magickal beyond measure to develop eyes to see that even Kings are just grown children in bigger bodies. And what does every child want more than anything?

Our pair of rents (parents), of course.

The ones who are neutral and do their part to stay that way as best as they can, oh how they get manipulated most by the ones who choose us as their host.

Only the darkness can take us over because we already are the light; the light we are.

The darkness makes us fear our own power and the true ones await guidance from the lady they trust to know best but when she is scared she can only add-vice.

Throughout the years the keepers of the sky have been the Khalessi's that tried to do it alone and drove themselves mad (as I seemed to be the day after this was written)…

What she needs are the ones who will stand true and tell her what she needs to hear, not just what she wants to hear because in her purity of heart she will think that she knows best.

The world order requires a reworking and those in power cannot afford it.

They have put all their chips on the dark side, without realizing it, choosing the black suits instead of the red. But no, they knew better when they went against their nature yet their inner sense did not stop trying to get through to them; that is our saving grace.

The red ones are the wisdom keepers who aspire to be so good they have set an impossible standard for themselves and this is what must fall.

The impossible ideal of perfectionism now needs to be released. Life is perfectly imperfect. It is time for us to realize that it is only with real eyes that we can trust what is true, in our heart of hearts and that is where the Earth comes in.

We got so scared we isolated and separated ourselves from the ones we deemed crazy. The ones who defied social convention and chose to do things according to what they felt to be right in their hearts even though it didn't seem we were playing our part in the machine we've been devoured by collectively.

They were prepared to face the consequences of that choice, even though they didn't fully understand, and so were we for we have all been playing our parts perfectly.

We need each other and when we try to do it alone we get scared, o so scared, because we know that isolation keeps us disconnected and less powerful than we could be together.

Well, what if it wasn't the Mother or Father who could keep the SUN safe at all?

What if they were merely the gatekeepers to bring forth the ones needing to interrupt the BS of our collective story so we can right/write our story in harmony together?

Let's start with the one that cripples us most: the story of 'not enough'

O yes, how the kind King Father does his best to sacrifice his own desires for the sake of his Mother and often ends up with a lady like the one who raised him (for we follow familiar patterns until we learn how to script new ones).

She will hold him while he cries and begs her to be strong for us all, and she will graciously accept the call because she knows she is the Mother of more than just her own.

Somehow parenthood unites us because the children force us to be present where we are and to leave the not-now in the past where it showed up to gift us a powerful lesson we may have yet to fully mine for its gold.

This is where our gifts and collective blessings come to the table, but first we must be willing to dig deep. Brene Brown's "*Gifts of Imperfection*" teaches that vulnerability and shame have become arch-nemesis' to each other because they know the battle within takes priority.

It's time to acknowledge how far we have come. How far we have travelled to get where we are, and to also trust ourselves to find the equal counterpart to our soul (not the ego) who can help us stay true to ourselves.

I've refrained from including the final lines of this story as I was battling demons and entities within I hadn't recognized then, yet the flow was genius (genie in us) and the veils were thin so the patterns reflect what I was facing within, thinking it was only without; I believe others can relate to the template we are now called to clear and recreate.

I thought it was about the snake's den as I called DC then but in retrospect I see how it forewarned of my own fall from grace in the race to awaken faster than I could handle that had started many months before.

Earlier that year I had been trying to 'storm the gates of heaven' by force using DMT, rapé and psilocybin mushrooms in ceremony with a Shaman, micro-dosing for a short stint, tried a 'hippie flip' that tripped me out, and I went on two three-week trips to Arizona (and area) in the name of 'breaking through' and making 'it' happen all of which contributed to my journey into insanity; by that I mean the system is insane because it treats the symptoms instead of the root cause of them, focusing on the mind when the emotions drive the fully equipped pharmacy within but that isn't my area of expertise so we'll leave it there. What I learned is that spiritual bypassing (trying to skip steps) means going through them backwards and like my mother says: "That is what you should not do, now let that be a lesson to you."

I joke about it now because if we can't laugh at ourselves then we'll take the jokes of others personally because we become too sensitive to the subtle truth at the foundation of every joke but there is a big difference between laughing at someone and laughing with them. Bullying ourselves only engrains the pattern which is precisely what the death cult promotes, along with quick fixes and fast rides that often cause more harm than good which is why I now choose to seek enlightenment naturally. That isn't to say I wouldn't partake in a plant ceremony ever again because ayahuasca, kambo and DMT are known to have entheogenic benefits that produce nonordinary states of consciousness but I am reluctant to give external entities access to and influence over my unconscious mind now that I've experienced the consequences of doing so.

I believe the integration of energies after such ceremonies are fundamental to the process of fully benefitting from them which was a missing piece in my puzzle. Energies in motion that get stirred too quick with this kind of external input can wreak havoc on one's grip with reality and resulting identity so must be treated with respect and reverence as the sacred teachers plant medicines are; disrespect them and prepare to face the karmic consequences, as I did.

Context is also important because it sheds light on where we've been and what (aspects of ourselves) we've faced which is why now I'll share that my 'awakening' experience was directly tied to the first three week sojourn earlier that year when I'd expanded and contracted energetically, and almost didn't survive myself emotionally upon my return. In some ways I believe the call that changed my life after writing the story above was my soul's way of saving me from a contracted state I don't know I could have survived without facing the beast head on; the mind is a trap and truth can be confusing in this inverted reality if we fail to face it directly.

After the eight DMT ceremonies I'd done between February and April of 2019, I got played hard by a woman my age who claimed to be a 'soul doula' who could help me rebirth myself naturally, as I had done in one of the ceremonies. Still riding the pattern of giving my power to others, I fronted the money for a three week sojourn to attend a conference in California with the same group I'd met in Tampa two years before. We started in Vegas, drove through Utah to Angel's Peak which was closed due to snow (quite symbolic), hiked up Cathedral Rock in Sedona, hit up Hollywood Hills with a villain character we'd met at the conference and wound up at a place called 'Wake House' for a couple days where I first heard about the legal fiction and the illusory foundation our current reality is based on. She milked me for as much as she could before another 'sucker' took over her tab and I drove back to Vegas alone while she stayed with a group I'd left on awkward terms. I was in the most expanded and confused state I'd experienced up to that point and the betrayal I felt bled out until forgiveness of myself for being deceived, used and manipulated helped me to heal the wound others preyed on after until I did.

When I returned home without having finished the book, with nothing but a speaking gig lined up that I'd tried to reschedule for an overlapping cruise I had a chance to work for a reduced ticket and far less money in my bank account from the whole experience, plus the cynical voices of those who reassured me that I wouldn't ever see the money owed to me, my mental health suffered. I got caught in a mind trap of my own making and shame, regret and disappointment for the way I'd left the group in California was part of it; subtle bullying had contributed and I fell into a downward spiral emotionally that was a hell of my own making.

I ended up cancelling everything using 'poor mental health' as my excuse but I'd lost money, opportunity, connections, energy, respect for myself and trust for others so was feeling pretty poor indeed. I was also conscious I had become an energetic drain on my parents and friends because I started feeding off of them to survive myself. It helped me see how our youth are being systematically targeted in this corrupted thought war where our energy is being fought for; when children drain their parents who are often providing for their parents, patrons at work, and community if actively involved, plus other family if applicable, it becomes too much and we shut down because we've got nothing left in the well to give. This is when society begins to collapse and we're seeing it en masse (as a whole).

May 2019 was the first time in my life that I lost hope in my ability to 'make it' as the creator of a life I loved living and I didn't know how to cope without hope.

The tell-a-vision played a reality that didn't seem real or resonant for me anymore and the projections of others seeing me 'floundering' who were trying to make an honest living while judging me for not doing so the usual way compounded the pressure I put on myself which only drove me deeper into a world of limiting BS. I had inadvertently become the spoiled brat I'd wrote about and needed to get grounded in real life again, after so much of my identity had got wrapped up in my online persona, but I couldn't figure out how to best do that.

It was a difficult time in my life and when I couldn't find a way out of the mental trap my disconnected lifestyle had created for me I wanted to die and was honest with those I loved about it. We turned to the Mental Health system and encountered the disheartening experience of being waitlisted for support because I had no intention to act on the suicidal ideations that consumed me while waiting for an appointment with a Psychiatrist.

Psychiatrist: a medical practitioner specializing in the diagnosis and treatment of mental illness. Former Psychiatrist William Glasser's book *WARNING: PSYCHIATRY CAN BE HAZARDOUS TO YOUR MENTAL HEALTH* was very insightful to me months later when I returned to the system, against my wishes, and no longer trusted the professional add-vice offered.

I was fortunate to have support from family who loved me and tried to help pull me out of the funk I was in then but had no clue that Addictions and Mental Health are presently treated separately within the system even though it's obviously directly connected. Funding is a corporate game and the ones needing help are forced to choose which problem to use their counselling for. It's insanity that reflects the vanity of dead entities that feed (profit) off people having problems.

Vanity: the quality of being worthless or futile.

I tried in vain to gain from the professional 'supports' I discovered from journeying into the user side of the mental health system in May 2019 and found it seriously lacking in substance because healthy people aren't as profitable for a corporate model designed to convert people into patients, addicts and dependents.

After a couple weeks, things started to line up for me and I got interviews for good positions that gave me something to look forward to which is what we all need to stay inspired. A friend also offered me a cheap room in his student house for the summer which gave me space to unfold in that was close enough to home I could visit and contribute without feeling trapped. It was exactly what I needed.

I was back on the horse and excited about life again, plus I started teaching English online part time and became a regular at the hot yoga studio in walking distance of my room. All the disappointments and hurtful experiences of feeling used, mistreated and confused about how to finish 'the book' faded to the background and I had energy to give back again knowing I was contributing to life instead of just taking. It was nice and also necessary for repairing my self-esteem and the way I saw myself.

Harboring resentment toward those who'd judged or used me for their own gain, including the vampiric system itself, opened me up to entities that took me down emotionally until I finally exercised the power of forgiveness and set myself free from entities I no longer choose to feed my energy to.

Forgiveness is not about forgetting what happened or letting someone take advantage of our kindness by letting it happen again. Forgiveness is about giving ourselves love and acceptance where another took advantage of the trust we gave them and now must take back. Separate the actor from the act and extract the fact (or lesson) you no longer wish to attract; that is how I have found forgiveness without being a doormat any longer.

Resentment keeps us from retrieving the lesson from the interaction we no longer wish to magnetize toward us and keeps us feeding the memory.

Forgive yourself for learning the hard way, recognize the pattern the other gave you an opportunity to face and clear the charge within you around, and call your power back from those who did you wrong. Not doing so keeps you in between them and their karma for what goes around comes around if we get ourselves out of the way by coming back present to play in a new way; we teach people how to treat us so use the past as contrast to get clear on what you want instead. So I thank those who gave me hard lessons I no longer wish to repeat and let them feel the loss of my presence in their lives for they helped me see my own value and that is priceless.

Don't let resentments fester or they'll keep you from the gift the present moment is.

Woundology, Recovery Of Self-Esteem & Rock Bottom States

7

I am a woman who has learned to take that power-full stand because when I lost my freedom under the Mental Health Act in 2019 I discovered that being on the other side of an order someone is paid to fulfill is not in my best interest.

What I also see is that if we do not stop living backwards as evil (live backwards literally) would have us do, then we are doomed whether we go out with a boom or not.

Ever since the last world war we have been taught to fear a nuclear war without seeing the symbolic, mythic and energetic connections between the nuclear family model or the 'just go nuke it' reference to microwaving things. We're in a nuclear war and our cells are the real e-state being fought for by corp-orations that need weak hosts to feed off of.

Our words are wands and if we're willing to consider the higher-level meanings behind the spells we cast with the words we spell out and then speak we'll start to see things in a new light without need to fight ourselves in the ways we have been.

Let's face it, the present REALITY we have been living in is based on lies piled on top of lies that get us to deny what we feel for the sake of what we're told is true.

The masks that have been mandated by corporations are a prime example and ones like myself who will not pretend to be other than our authentic selves have lost out on opportunities awarded to those willing to play by the rules and con-form.

In the months that followed my release from the system that tried to convert me into a profit-able party (patient) it could feed off, I was forced to rebuild my life without the support of the system or many who I'd thought would be there for me but weren't. This is where I realized that when lighthouses fall, boats get out of the way and as one willing to shine my light despite the fight waging war within, I recognized the need to find others who could relate to the ostracism I experienced in a heightened way when dealing with those fully invested in the literal world and closed off to the mythic, symbolic and energetic realms.

It's the Old World versus the Newly Ordered World that is NOW coming to be.

Caroline Myss was a big influence in my understanding of mysticism and energy and really helped me see how we've been conditioned to bond through our traumas and dramas using what she refers to as 'woundology' where we compare wounds as a way to bond and connect. And if what I went through wasn't intense enough on its own, the aftermath of it and another private matter led me to break down instead of breakthrough in February 2020 when I finally bought the bull I'd been sold about my 'outlandish' ways.

I'd continued teaching English online and making videos to empower and inspire others while fighting to figure out how to come back from my 'public fall' and for irony and experience sake I became a 'Mad Scientist' briefly until the pressure of all I'd been through and the judgements of ones I respected became too much for me to bear.

My WEB of self-worth, self-esteem, and self-belief imploded and I no longer wanted to live if I couldn't be me without putting profits before people, yet I couldn't pull the plug either. I felt like a complete failure and took the projections of loved ones personally who told me I would never finish the book I'd put so much emphasis on and needed to retrain and find a job, like they had. Others who had always been in my corner, had been hurt by me and lost trust in me, and we no longer had an open line of communication or trust which hurt my heart in an indescribable way.

In February 2020 I called the local Crisis Stabilization Bed Program I'd discovered from my experiences, and checked myself in for five days while at the lowest point I'd ever experienced. And in so doing I lost my teaching contract and quit being a Mad Scientist.

I had reached what felt like rock bottom and as J.K Rowling famously said "Rock bottom became the solid foundation on which I rebuilt my life."

After leaving that place convinced the mental health system is not designed to help the ones in desperate need of compassionate care beyond their stay, I decided to surrender to the Universe and applied for some minimum wage paying jobs because that was all I felt capable of. When the local Superstore called to set up an interview I was elated, and still recovering from the cold I'd developed when I gave up on myself and went through a cellular upgrade which is what we do when we uplevel; I've never been tested for a virus that's never been isolated so cannot confirm nor deny I've ever had 'it' (whatever that means).

My ego had been hit hard and my sense of self-worth was in the gutter, along with my self-esteem and self-belief, but getting offered the position of cashier in the interview was the start of my come back and I am grateful. I remember having seen a message earlier that day to accept unexpected offers so when the offer was made I accepted with gratitude, without any idea that my country was about to go through what my Chinese students had been experiencing already for several months.

A Cashier Standing For Truth On 'The Frontlines'

8

I don't think the group of new hires I was in had even finished our training when the area manager appeared the night before Good Friday to let us know someone at our store had tested positive for 'the virus' and it was closing early to be fumigated over the holiday. What convenient timing I'd thought while silently questioning what fumigation of the store meant from a health perspective, but I didn't want to seem 'too out there' in my new position so early on so I didn't ask too many questions.

Most days for the ten months I worked there I was scheduled for short four hour shifts that absorbed my focus, as most part time employees are in the grocery business. And so it was that each shift I showed up to interact with people from all walks of life to find out what was happening in our community and the lives of the people in it.

It didn't take long for me to see how we suddenly had a higher status than our pay grade had previously warranted because for a time we even received 'danger pay' for being willing to continue showing up on the 'frontlines' when some had surrendered their position in fear of an invisible enemy. I also saw how some of my colleagues thrived on the added power they perceived themselves to have by being able to 'direct traffic' when the lines got long and greater distance between customers was supposedly required; there was only one really, but she left a bad taste in many mouths for it, including my own.

When I got put on traffic duty I acted like Vanna White to make it a fun experience for those I directed to the next available till and when I was on the till I locked eyes with those who came through to call them present and break them out of the fear spell all around us, letting them know I cared for we all just want to be seen and feel we matter. It was sacred work I took seriously, because I also used the opportunity to inquire how much people knew about the Agendas I'd read were behind it all.

Many thought me to be a conspiracist theorist and some colleagues were rude and dismissive toward me by the end, but I didn't care and felt I was there for a significant reason.

I joked with some customers and colleagues that I was part of the 're-training brigade' who was there to tell them where they could stand during each stage of the check-out experience which for a time was quite ridiculous, as many may recall.

I did my best to make it fun and recognized the insanity I'd experienced behind closed doors had now entered the public sphere in a covert and subtle way, with excuses to justify it all. For that is what victims do: blame, complain, justify and deny.

Wearing a mask was not an option I was willing to accept because I recognized how psychologically traumatizing it is to those who see one willing to wear (someone else's) fear on their face when a mask to defend oneself against a virus is like putting up a fence to keep out a mosquito. It would have also taken away one of my greatest spell breakers which is the universal language of care a genuine smile conveys.

When masks were mandated province wide days after I'd made a cheeky post from Port Burwell's nude beach where I'd used my arm and a frisbee to maintain my modesty, in the name of no tan lines, I was conflicted. I'd been speaking up the whole time but when I was told I had to go to the office to sign an exemption form I felt the pressure we all did.

The woman serving as my Doctor at the time had declined my need for an exemption, due to her own beliefs, and so it was that I felt coerced to at least agree to wear a shield for the first few shifts afterward. But when a supervisor that disliked me told me I had to keep the shield below my chin I had the equivalent of a panic attack because there was no way I was going to wear someone else's fear in accordance with rules I didn't believe in.

I returned to the office and re-signed my exemption form, assuming authority for my own health choices despite the consequences I knew would come but I no longer feared. I recognized that every opportunity comes into our lives for a reason, season or lifetime and I'd only taken the job when I did because of all I'd been through; I also believe I was sent there to be an ambassador for truth for as long as I could stay, so I did, until January 15, 2021 when I was forced into an unpaid leave of absence effective at the end of that shift.

Corporations are part of this attempted corporatocratic takeover because they can change their corporate by-laws to impose rules on their patrons and employees once its been pre-scripted into their policies. In order for the next waves of the Pendemic to fly, those unwilling to 'go along to get along' must be removed early on in 'the game' to ensure those who stay have already bought into the BS that becomes more forceful each time the line is pushed. This is part of the way the herd has been trained to maintain itself and the details were laid out at *Event 201*.

Monkeys, Maslow & Robbins' Motivational Needs Theories

9

There was a famous monkey experiment that exemplifies the pattern of the "herd mentality" we've seen playing out throughout this Pendemic that is appropriate to share in the ninth chapter; a number of endings which leads to new beginnings.

A group of monkeys were put into a habitat where a tall tree with bananas at the top was placed in the centre. The first monkey to notice them climbed up the tree to get the bananas and right before he reached the top he got sprayed until he fell down and everyone down below got wet too.

That monkey was then removed from the experiment and replaced by another monkey who saw the bananas and raced to the top to get them but experienced the same fate and once again the monkeys below got wet too.

That monkey was taken out and replaced by another who tried the same but was roughly pulled back down by one of the monkeys below who had seen the other two get sprayed and refused to let that monkey go up.

One by one each of the original monkeys were removed from the habitat and replaced by other monkeys who all tried for the bananas but were all pulled back down before they even had a chance to get sprayed. Eventually only monkeys who had been pulled back by other monkeys remained in the habitat.

Even though none of them had personally been impacted by or witnessed another monkey get sprayed on the way to the bananas, when a new monkey was brought in who tried to go for the bananas it too was pulled back by those who had been warned of the threat by others and were pulled back before they'd had a chance to try either.

"Fair's fair" many would say, but how does that help our cause when so many are living at the effect end of the cause and effect equation? The obvious answer is that it doesn't, purposefully, for disempowered people, or monkeys, are easier to control and manipulate by the few who have power because so many give up before they've even really tried.

Generations of victims have been caught in toxic WEBs like this, designed to 'stay safe' at the expense of significance and so it is with the majority of us too.

We've been raised hearing the horror stories of trauma, drama and loss others experienced when they stepped out of their comfort zone and 'went for it' (whatever that 'it' may be) and then argue for their limitations to intimidate and impose them on others to keep the playing field level. Yet no longer can we afford to stay hunched over to support a game board only the privileged few get a chance to play while the majority suffer and pay the price of entertaining entitled fools with no real skin in the game.

FEAR has been used to keep us in contracted states, playing small in order to conform and fit roles we've been raised to believe we must compete for with others; we forgot that we are originals and were each born with unique gifts, designed for a specific purpose that only we can fulfill, regardless of where our journey began or what resources were available to us then.

Our EGO is the 'Edging God Out' part of us that can only see life through the lens of our humanly self while our higher self can see the whole picture if only we are willing to listen to the in-sights it is always offering from the silence. Our higher self is omnipresent and unlimited by the circumstances we see with our five senses; it has access to senses beyond the constraints of our 3D REALITY which is where the opinions of others live.

From the outset of the pre-scripted Pendemic the mainstream narrative has relied on denials and False Emotion Appearing Real using propaganda that has promoted compliance with unhealthy and unnatural regulations in the name of building 'herd immunity' to protect the weak and vulnerable; like the proverb says "the road to hell is paved with good intentions."

Abraham Maslow's *Hierarchy of Motivational Needs theory* must now be considered in relation to Tony Robbins' equivalent but slightly different theory, using the monkey experiment and Pandemic as prime examples of how individualism has been trumped by collectivism.

Individualism: the habit or principle of being independent and self-reliant.

Collectivism: the practice or principle of giving a group priority over each individual in it.

By: Laura JE Hamilton

Comparative Hierarchy of Motivational Needs
Theories: Abraham Maslow vs Tony Robbins.

Maslow's theory suggests that we are motivated by priority needs before being able to see 'the bigger picture' of what is available to us. Survival is at the foundation with physiological needs (food, shelter, water, sex) coming before safety, belonging, respect or self-actualization. In the monkey experiment, the monkeys had their primary needs met so the bananas were seen as an unnecessary indulgence once the pursuit of them caused harm or discomfort to those on the ground or who had dared to try.

In the context of this Pendemic, priority has been given to safety and survival with belonging used as a tool to shame any self-respecting individuals into compliance by exclusion and downright ostracism, as many of us have experienced firsthand. Self-actualization or 'making the most of oneself' has been left out of the mainstream narrative altogether for it requires creators be re-actors instead.

Robbins' theory is similar but he suggests certainty comes before variety, connection, significance, growth and contribution which build upon one another. He also says that our need for certainty, variety, connection and significance can be met through violence and psychopathic tendencies like we've seen playing out on the public stage throughout this whole psy-op. It's connected to the increasing number of school shootings too because growth and contribution seem out of reach to one hypnotized by lower levels, and that is by design.

Not our natural design, might I add, but the design of those who pre-scripted the terrorism current-lie being imposed by de facto governments who only have power because we, the people, have been conditioned to give ours to them and live by default as a result. It's insanity by Einstein's definition which is to do the same thing while expecting different results.

Einstein is also quoted to have said that we cannot solve problems with the same level of thinking that created them, and so it is that we must lift our individual and collective focus to a higher level so that belonging to a toxic culture no longer resonates because we've 'raised the bar' energetically, which is what consciousness is.

It is said that only a small percentage of the population are responsible for holding the balance in consciousness which is why so many lighthouses feel so alone during dark times and require support the system cannot afford to offer. The current system profits off of dysfunction because dis-regulated people turn to professionals for solutions that fail to address the underlying emotional cause of their problems; energy in motion needs to move and suppressing things only builds pressure over time. Eventually the pressure will grow and need to be expressed which will not be comfortable after holding back for so long.

We need to equip ourselves to support one another through these uncomfortable moments without taking them personally or trying to offer solutions or add-vice that add pressure to one already imploding under the weight of maintaining false appearances that keep us weak and divided. We also need to look beyond the nuclear family model that is ill-equipped to support the weight of emotional burdens when so much has been buried over time that many do not wish to disturb, discuss or have exposed.

While many within the communities we live in will not only be disinterested in this kind of information but will also try to dissuade you from giving it any credence like the monkeys that pulled back others aiming for higher heights than they'd managed to achieve themselves, it is your response-ability to feel your way through these words to see how they sit and fit for you. You may wish to refrain from discussing your engagement with this work until you've become more familiar with its contents and the emotional spectrum it will help you maneuver more consciously but question everything and let your feelings be your guide without trying to hide what is showing up to be healed through self-acceptance.

Collective consciousness is impacted by every one of us and the more soul fragments we are willing to call back by moving the energies in motion so we can be pre-sent where we are without the emotional disturbances of suppressed energies is a great contribution, even if no one else can tell how much we're doing for the collective as we heal from the inside out.

Another monkey experiment that epitomizes the tipping point in collective consciousness we are each contributing to whether consciously or unconsciously is often referred to as the 100th Monkey Effect.

It started with a group of monkeys living on an island who were fed a diet of sweet potatoes, delivered to the beach each day.

One day one of the sweet potatoes rolled into the water and a nearby monkey retrieved it, washed it off in the water, and discovered that doing so removed the grit beached potatoes always had on them. So it did what social creatures do; it showed monkeys it knew about this newly discovered secret to better tasting sweet potatoes and they all did the same with monkeys they knew until someone told the hundredth monkey and suddenly all monkeys everywhere knew to wash their sweet potatoes.

The awareness had become part of the collective consciousness that was available to all monkeys and while one hundred will not necessarily be the 'magic number' for us, many sacred texts have suggested 144,000 is the equivalent that will help us shift to a higher level of consciousness collectively. Yet what if that didn't actually have anything to do with anyone outside of each of us?

What if that tipping point number reflected the aspects of ourselves we're able and willing to reclaim in the name of be-coming pre-sent in the NOW moment where all of our creative power exists?

What if instead of trying to tell people about all the ugly truths that are available for them to see if they wanted to look, we shifted our approach and focused on changing our energetic signature to feel more PEACE-FULL despite the insanity all around us? And from this charged state of pre-sense we united forces to create a vision that feels trust-worthy and sustain-able for those who will inherit the world we are creating now?

What if we remembered the power-full distinction between being in charge of our energy versus trying to control ourselves and others in a universe based on free will?

Words will not change the minds of those unwilling to believe we've all been deceived by the authorities they've tied their identities to, yet the example of one vibrating at a higher level that feels better than all the FEAR-FULL presentations of REALITY current-lie available is undeniable because it can be felt. Peace, truth, love, joy and empowerment is resonant and feels good because it is pure.

As energetic beings we read energy automatically, without a 'one size fits all' manual that doesn't actually fit all at all. We resonate with truth and feel unsteady or uncertain around mis-truths we can't explain; it's simply our inner guidance system letting us know when something is 'off' and not vibrating at the level of truth. But how do we explain that to one who wants to rationalize truth with a 'ration of lies' they need us to buy from them for their profit?

Until we become safe havens for others to turn to energetically, we unintentionally contribute to the problem because the 'ugly truth' is not a viable solution unless we band together to create a vision that feels better than the lies told by the 'tell a vision' so many have faithfully invested energy into knowing, thinking it was the truth.

It is time for us to prioritize a relationship with the energies in motion within us that are reflected by one another until we own them by integrating their lessons without fearing them.

Let us do the impossible and rise above the tyranny by letting the energies in motion within us rise to the surface without judgement so that we can heal from the trauma those energies want to re-mind us to beware of. It's time to call ourselves present in more functional ways and see the "I'm possible" in what we previously believed to be impossible.

As energetic beings having a physical experience we must see how our energetic signature speaks for us and do our part to integrate the lessons our emotions show up to gift us with and then let them go without attachment to the not-now moment it re-minds us of. This is how we empower ourselves to be present and contribute by showing up fully present with those who will feel us to be safe guides for the healing process they must go through too.

"Your energy speaks so loud I can't hear what you're saying."

Knowledge and information are not the dots we need to connect; we are the light (dots) that need no words to find common ground if we are willing to be truly pre-sent where we are, with whom we are there with. For as many have been quoted to say: "yesterday is history, tomorrow is a mystery, today is a gift that's why it's call the present."

The Rally, Magna Carta & Self-Presentation That Called Me Pre-Sent

10

On April 10, 2021 I was guided to attend an anti-lockdowns rally that indirectly called me back to life a couple weeks later when my person was summoned for acting out of turn in an Act I never agreed to play in; before then I recognized the SYSTEM was dangerous to ones who see through the false front of 'Saving You Significant Time Energy Money' yet I hadn't lived the experience I now have that has helped me see the need to not only be authentic but to claim the right to lawfully self-govern as a woman in my private capacity at all times, even when maneuvering through public spaces, as I now have and will continue to do as long as I am living.

The night before I'd got together with a group of local women concerned about the cultural perversions we'd seen playing out during the first year of the Pendemic. We met up at a local restaurant that was defying mandates by remaining open without requiring masks and had an enjoyable evening connecting and getting to know one another and the families some had brought along with them.

They invited me to the next day's rally a few of them intended to attend, but I declined in accordance with Mother Theresa's powerful sentiment: "I will never attend an anti-war rally. If you have a peace rally, invite me."

When I returned home I went to bed with a full heart, questioning how I was going to 'be the change I seek in this world' presuming it would be through the virtual PEACE Summits I'd been arranging with friends I felt people could benefit from hearing. But around

3am I woke up knowing I needed to go to the rally and see if I could speak on stage.

I messaged my lady-friends and coordinated to meet them at the rally and set out to accomplish the mission I felt had been placed on my heart in the night.

We found one another upon arrival and positioned ourselves in the packed crowd, ironically in the parking lot opposite where I'd been forced out as a cashier months earlier, and then I made my way to the front to find out how I might get myself on stage.

The first man I approached 'happened' to be one of the organizers so I introduced myself and grabbed his details so I could be in touch about speaking at the next one given it was a full roster with a couple 'big names' I recognized. The insecure part of me didn't want to be an inconvenience and I somehow perceived that requests to speak on stage were more common than may actually be true; my experience with the JMT and other speaking related trainings I'd attended over the years gave me a biased belief that wanting to speak publicly was a shared goal for many. I had forgot public speaking is one of the most common phobias people suffer from.

Feeling excited by the prospect of speaking at the next one I returned to my friends to hear the lineup of speakers and after a couple speeches one of my friends challenged me saying "you know who I'd love to hear speak up there? (pause for dramatic effect) YOU! Go try again."

The reasonable part of me momentarily contested because "I'd already tried" but the willful part of me won out, knowing I'd come with a last minute assignment to do my best to get up there. So I weaved my way back up to the front, to the man I knew could help me make it happen if anyone there could, and asked "so, any chance I could get up there today?"

He reached out to the MC who was standing nearby and asked "can she get up there?" The MC shrugged and said "why not? Just be short and sweet because Randy Hillier's up next." And so minutes later as the man speaking at the time finished and handed the mic back to the MC he introduced me without even knowing my name and gave me the floor.

I wasn't prepared, I didn't have a speech, I didn't know what I was going to say but I did my best and got out of my own way so I could be the vessel I felt I'd been sent there to be. And I didn't immediately judge myself when I got off stage either because I remembered a story one of my early author-influences, Louise Hay, had shared from her own experience; find something to celebrate yourself for before getting out the scalpel of constructive criticism that kills courage in future moments when you will be called to step up again.

Was it the best speech that day? For sake of reference to the stallion story earlier I'll say 'maybe?' but what mattered to me most was that a little girl came up to me afterwards, excited to meet me and to thank me for speaking. I had touched her heart which is exactly what was and is required now, especially within the future leaders of this world we share.

I shared several disjointed perspectives that day including the need for 'blue pillers' to wake up 'blue pillers' who are willing to listen to 'red pillers' who've went further down rabbit holes to see how all the 'conspiracy theories' connect to the legitimate conspiracy behind this whole psy-op. For at the time I was still sub-scribed to many of the freedom movements propagating FEAR in a different package because until we get back to the basics, as men and women, it's all too easy to create camps of righteousness for 'us' versus 'them' when we're all playing roles within the same field of consciousness here on the plan-et(ation) called Earth.

Our energy is being harvested to varying degrees by corps(e) that feed off our False Emotion Appearing Real and confine will-full ones who don't buy the poisoned mainstream narrative as easily as those willing to settle down and fall in line with the rest; like in the movie *Monsters Inc* where laughter produces more energy but cannot be harvested by the machines in the same way FEAR can be, we must lift our voices to sing in harmony within this Uni-verse to em-power ourselves instead of the machine or corporate entities preying on our energy.

There is no us versus them when we all bleed red until corporate forms leave us black and blue, as the colours of ink used to seal our fate if not aware that purple is the colour of sovereign souls who claim the right not to be -under ('sous' in French) -ver ('right' in French) -reign (rule as king or queen) of a corps(e) that contracts our substance to fit its forms.

I knew my choice would come with consequences but the day itself was relatively uneventful after the speakers wrapped up and the crowds got marching orders to draw more attention to protestations against the unlawful mandates those present saw need to defeat.

Aside from making some good connections and 'feeling the vibes' physical proximity permits in a way video can't convey, it seemed relatively uneventful. But a couple weeks later when a man acting as a POLICE Officer showed up 'to deliver paperwork' I did not accept, but he left on the porch anyway, I under-stood why I'd been sent.

My experience getting locked up against my will in 2019 and being denied access to a lawyer without a psychiatrist's approval made me unwilling to be represented by someone who was not 'in it' with me. And what I experienced first-hand as a patient, and had seen in professional situations too, is that it's easy for words to be misconstrued by those paid to document activities we take for granted until they are limited and we learn their true value.

I wasn't sure what I was going to do about this implied charge but I knew the 'predictive programming' outlined in *Event 201* aimed to target those willing to speak up with fines and jail time that drained those with resources early on so by the time the warriors were taken out of circulation the rest were easier to corral and control.

While that was my first oration to a crowd locally I had been speaking out online for years and had even started a podcast to interview people I saw had uncommon knowledge others would benefit from. When my friend got involved with the *Practical Lawful Dissent International group* that David Robinson had formed and organized before his untimely death in November 2020, she sent me an interview of the self-assumed leader who went by the alias of Jacquie Phoenix. I contacted her for an interview and she agreed in

December 2020 where she shared the five-step notice process David had created to put the cops, courts and councils on notice of the de facto government's overreach of power; 25 Barons are said to have evoked Article 61 of the 1215 Magna Carta on March 23, 2001 which has yet to be remedied which means the Government have been operating unlawfully ever since then, if not before.

Because the paperwork was hard to understand without a legal background I asked Jacquie to attend a "Lawfully Organized Summit" I hosted to help people feel more confident about moving forward, myself included. She agreed and my biggest takeaway was learning the difference between a notice and a letter which was a vital foundation for dealing with the implied charge against my person. My friend and I ended up hosting twelve such meetings in total trying to gain clarity before disconnecting from the movement as "where there is only one way in and out, it's generally a trap" and I am concerned for those following that initiative.

It was around the time when drama between key individuals within that movement, and mixed jurisdictions within the paperwork, led me to disconnect with slightly more insight into alternative options than I'd had before. But when the man acting as an officer came to 'deliver paperwork' I remembered that this group had suggested recording any interactions with POLICE on my phone as he was the man I could see which means that he is liable for fulfilling the order to commit fraud against me; plausible deniability is the corporate excuse to limit liability of employees but if we take the suit off the man acting as an employee, or any other fiction, the corps(e) can no longer cover the man for we all act of our own accord. Better to own our faults now than take them to the grave where our soul will pay the price in our next life.

We must begin to see the connection between the eye 'i' can see and the corporate entity that uses men and women to do its dirty work on its be-half. I knew I was in a bind I had to find a way out of but I also trusted that I would not have been sent if I could not get out of the trap set for myself and my fellow men and women to fall into unawares, as I had under the Mental Health Act that is nothing short of evil.

While working at the grocery store I'd made a couple friends from conversations with patrons I resonated with, one of whom was a man taking on the municipal government for interfering with the course of justice over his son's hit and run several years before. The details aren't mine to share but in the summer of 2020 he revealed some of the systemic corruption we're currently facing which relates to the "C'est qui vie Trust Act" of 1666 where we were all legally declared dead and lost at sea; this is how we're implied to be under the jurisdiction of Admiralty/Maritime Law. It's also why hospitals stamp a baby's foot print, to show it walked on their land (form) first and thus became property of the owner of the form. But I digress…

During one drop-in I felt called to make after I'd finished my shift at the store, he had a friend painting his living room who came out to sit in on our conversation for a short time. He told me about his 'Thrivalism' concept which is a similar concept to GESARA/NESARA which I'd heard Michael Seegers talk about in the work we were doing together at that time for "The Michael & Laura Show" which helped me see how entities feed off of those who pray to an outer force (and ultimately become energetic prey to it).

The man painting that day was Neil Sperling and the next spring when I received that summons I had no idea how grateful I would be for that 'coincidental' connection that day.

When I got improperly served by the first man acting as a police officer in April 2021 I went back to the only man I knew personally who was handling his own legal matters. His first recommendation was to take down the footage of me speaking that I'd found online and copied, as someone working for the police had also done. Denying what I believed I had every right to do was not a viable solution but I needed help and he was my best option until the day after when he indirectly helped me find a safer way forward which we all have the right to claim and stand on as men and women on common ground (common law).

The Capitalizing Of LAW
Lacking In Heart

11

Neil had called our mutual friend for something else who was excited about 'our case' for which I am ultimately grateful because of who else Neil knew could legitimately help me. When Neil then reached out to see if I wanted to be introduced to the man I've come to call 'my law man' all the pieces I'd been picking up from the mental health system, coercion within my workplace, all the 'lawful dissent' meetings I'd hosted and the material David Robinson had put together started to paint a fuller picture.

What was missing was the uncommon approach my law man had learned over decades of private study and offering assistance to friends who'd rubbed up against the corrupted system that converts men and women into a lesser status, as I've since learned and am practicing using given my pre-trial hearing is now just days away.

It has truly been the most empowering process I've ever experienced because it helped me see how what happened to me in 2019 was legal (not lawful) and why, I believe, I got Divinely sent to that rally with friends who encouraged me to do what I wouldn't necessarily have done on my own. This is how rescuers become challengers that uplift and empower.

It's the reason I say that my summons brought me back to life and why I am forever grateful to all three of these men for helping me see where we've went off track collectively.

Having their emotional support along the way has also been invaluable and is more relevant to you than 'my story' might suggest. Here's why.

The group of ladies I'd met up with at the rally shared a lot of alternative resources and one that stood out for me was an interview Sasha Stone did with Anna von Reitz and two others. I took extensive notes and learned about the Charter of the Forest 1225 which is said to be the accompanying charter to the 1215 Magna Carta that had received so much of my attention in the months before. Admittedly I dropped that ball shortly afterwards because I didn't know to use it or how it could be applied to my own case which required my focus.

That interview was also where I learned that the court of LAW represents multiple jurisdictions; juris meaning 'of right; of law' and diction meaning 'what is spoke or wrote' which is why in a court of LAW we're asked "do you under-stand?" as a covert way to say we stand under their jurisdiction.

LAW can thus be seen as an acronym for multiple jurisdictions running simultaneously:

L = Land is where men and women stand on common ground under 'common law' which is the unwritten and unlimited law of conscience and morality, based on not causing harm, loss or fraud to our fellow man. Violations here lead to criminal complaints and charges, just beware there is no capitalizing of letters, for 'Common Law' and 'common-law' are written and therefore limited versions of the original.

A = Air represents ecclesiastical law or 'Canon Law' which is the collection of rules imposed by authority granted power by the people who believe in the author-i-tie my identity to outside of themselves. Canon law refers to the body of ecclesiastical law that developed within Christianity, particularly Roman Catholicism, governing the internal hierarchy and administration of the church. To say the church and state are separate is a myth.

W = Water represents Maritime and Admiralty law which are used interchangeably to cover a variety of cases including contracts, torts, injuries, and other offenses that take place on any navigable water. The Crown is the equivalent to a pirate ship and we are presumed to be '(in)mates' until we take back our power as the authority of our own lives and claim the right to live in the land of benefits instead of the seas of liabilities.

When we claim the right to remain in our private capacity at all times, as I have done for a year trying to deal with an implied charge I do not consent to, we are not bound by public mandates, legislation or rules imposed by any jurisdiction in the public and any man or woman who claims otherwise must take the stand without corporate protection to prove they have a superior claim; if they cannot (or will not) the claim stands and no corps(e) can stand on its own. That's why those wearing suits to act on be-half of corp-orations must read the policies and procedures manual their position binds them by and to while working on its be-half.

What many trying to use a 'common law' argument are not aware of is how CAPITIS DIMINUTIO (a diminishing or abridgment of personality) has been used to create divisions of 'Common Law' that limit it and those using it without clarifying that true 'common law' is unwritten and therefore unlimited. 'English Common Law' and "King's Common Law" are written and therefore limited forms of the original which is what the legal fiction is based on.

Capitis diminutio maxima, media and minima are forms of 'capitalizing' on *Ignorantia juris non excusat* or *ignorantia legis neminem excusat* (Latin for "ignorance of the law excuses not" and "ignorance of law excuses no one" respectively) which is a legal principle holding that a person who is unaware of a law may not escape liability for violating that law merely by being unaware of it. Is it any wonder the media, or medium capitalization through conversion of one thing into another, is the commonly used method for propagating the lies?

Notice that all written laws refer to a 'person' or 'human' which are perversions of the original man or woman; this ties directly to the transhumanism agendas currently influencing legislation and education (indoctrination) programming given our youth are being targeted and our elders intentionally taken out of circulation so their wisdom goes with them to the grave.

Everything matters in the eyes of the LAW and the legal system is based on lie-ability which is intentionally soul destroying, and why lawyers are referred to as "devil's advocates" for they are working for a system that lived backwards while good men and women did nothing to address the core problem, until we did because we are now.

It is significant to note the connection between 'core problem' and the French word for heart which is 'coeur' (pronounced like core). For the legal fiction and corrupted system have become heartless in the race to climb the corporate ladder which often encourages people to use others in order to get a-head; just like when the letter i is capitalized and the head is boxed in, like a coffin we didn't know a rut would put us into.

Priorities, FEAR & Walking In The Dark

12

I first heard John C. Maxwell say that the only difference between a rut and a grave is that a rut has both ends kicked out. It made sense and is why so many people feel caught in the rat race that is not leading to fulfillment or self-actualization in the way we came here to experience life.

The quest for status and profits has led many to an early grave and the stress of trading our life for a job that fills the bank account while depleting the soul makes Mondays a day statistically more probable for heart attacks to occur, according to an article in 'The New York Times' from 2006.

Lifestyle choices naturally play into this as well but it's reasonable to say we didn't come here to trade our lives to fulfill someone else's vision; this also ties to the 'mid-life crisis' phenomenon of waking up at a perceived 'half-way point' to realize you ticked all the boxes you thought you were supposed to but somehow still find something to be missing. That sense of urgency to share the song in your heart with the world while you're here rears its head to remind you that life is not a dress rehearsal.

We only get one shot at this life as us, regardless of whether you believe in reincarnation or not; you'll never get to be the same version of you that you are NOW in another REALITY which is based on Realistic Evidence Appearing Legit In Tomorrow's Yesterday. So that re-mind-(h)er comes to the forefront of your mind that time in a death cult is limited, given the aim and emphasis of it.

This is also why the graveyard is said to be the richest place in the world, full of the unsung heart songs of those who left before they shared their gifts with the world.

John also says that our priorities show up in our chequebook and calendar because what we make time for is what we demonstrate is most important to us, through our actions. "Your actions speak so loud I can't hear what you're saying" is a good reflection of this truth which we must relearn how to feel within the bodies we have so often taken for granted until we experience a problem.

But we've all heard the saying "an ounce of prevention is worth a pound of cure" and so it is that we must understand our place within creation and why taking back our power as co-creators of the world we share is vital at this time in our shared story.

It's significant to point out that the court of LAW is not pluralized because the S is said to represent 'Space (and time)' which are the creator's territory; creations can only own their own creations, not the creator of them.

The Hierarchy of Creation is the most concise demonstration of our true place in life, before the SYSTEM corrupted our cell-F image to believe we are just cogs in a dysfunctional wheel as so many have come to think. That play on self-image connects to the fact that we can either choose to fill our cells with FEAR or faith which naturally impact our perception of ourselves, the world and our place within it.

I believe that we came here to no longer deceive others by coming clean as to how we've allowed ourselves to be corrupted in the name of belonging, buying respect and seeming to self-actualize through things instead of treasuring who we've been, are becoming through the journey of life and who we've loved in the process, for love is the whole point. That's not to say money is bad because as the buy-bull says "it is the love of money that is evil," but that's because faith has been filtered through a lens of FEAR and now it is time to draw near the fire of our own hearts again, as was always intended. We just got confused as to which re-legion to pledge allegiance to in order to gain access to the truth that would set us free; the truth is that no book will give you everything you need because it's about learning how to feel our way through the darkness of our own emotions instead of piling ourselves higher with others' BS we don't feel good enough in relation to because it's not ours but we're trying to act like it is.

Many orators have said the acronym for FEAR is False Evidence Appearing Real but I dare to say we must take that a layer deeper and see that FEAR is False Emotion Appearing Real in the NOW when we feel all the momentums of suppression that emerge in the moment to be healed. If we're in FEAR we won't be able to hear the unspoken truths of the perpetual NOW.

It's like the story about when FEAR was walking in the dark and saw a house with lights in the distance it came to overtake. To frighten the home owner it made scary noises all around before then knocking on the door, but when faith answered there was no one there. For faith and FEAR cannot coexist within the same space and if we'll allow ourselves to feel fully, without judgement of what is showing up to be healed and integrated, love will all-ways win.

Networking, Bad Add-Vice & OPCA Litigant Status Conversion Threats

13

After receiving the summons in April 2021, I started networking within the freedom movement in Canada and got quite caught up in a number of weekly calls using the PEACEFULL INNER Warriors United initiative as a way to find and assemble lighthouses who were willing to do the INNER work while shining bright on our respective turfs (communities and networks).

For months I invested countless hours into weekly "leader's meetings" while also sitting on a spiritual outreach committee because of the work I'd done to create and produce a series that disseminated the proclaimed teachings of the 'ascended masters' by Summit Lighthouse that I was trying to gather information about, hence creating the show. I was also hosting virtual 'PEACE Summits' and workshops to bring progressive thinkers together in the name of rising above the external chaos of the modern day, and I co-led and launched a music project called Album22 that brought artists from around the globe together at a time when touring was off limits, plus I was sharing my insights along the way as I worked privately with my law man to clear my name and protect myself from the unlawful imposition of de facto laws I do not believe are in the greatest or highest good of the people for whom they are said to be made. I was doing a lot but wasn't getting paid because I believed warriors need to be able to find one another more than I needed a bank account full of fiat currency that will be worthless when the markets crash and people lose their minds because the lies will no longer be deniable.

Unfortunately, people often only value things in relation to their investment into them so my efforts to make my words accessible to people who may not have paid for it devalued my efforts and drained my own energetic resources due to an imbalanced reciprocal exchange of energy. I knew better but my WEB (of self-Worth, Esteem and Belief) kept me from doing better until I recognized the value of calling back my energy so I could direct it more intentionally.

I felt significant because of my involvement with these groups and the caliber of people I was meeting because of it all but I began to feel an aspect of energy harvesting by having to repeat my story and view of the solution because I was too distracted to get it written down in a way that others could get to and through when they were ready to receive it. Fire hosing people with information is overwhelming for both parties so after my cat's death I committed to cleaning up my act so I could help in a practical way and this book is the result.

We've always been taught connecting the dots was about information when what I've learned is that we must come into formation and stand together as men and women, for united we stand, divided we fall, especially within our cells above all.

Before disengaging I was trying to share my alternative perspective as to how we could 'turn this ship around' through personal liability which I'd learned requires us take the suits off the men and women wearing them, metaphorically speaking. For titles, statuses and personages protect the men and women acting under the corporate umbrella only so long as the men and women are 'covered' from personal liability by their position. This is exactly what I was doing in my own case, I just didn't have an out-come yet to back up my claims and I was explaining my point of view to lawyers, doctors and corporate executives who couldn't believe what I was saying to be true, or didn't want to admit it given their private alliances and allegiances; hidden hands they'd aligned with and not shared publicly.

I'll always remember the private conversation I had with a leader trying to expose the myth behind Canada's formation who agreed to converse with me after a group call where his add-vice was recommended to me. We spoke the next day and I told him what I'd done up to that point with my lawful notices which was prior to my first scheduled hearing; his advice shocked me.

He told me that if I didn't attend the hearing, which I'd claimed the right not to do in my notices, the corporation of Canada would send out its corporate dogs to arrest me, which is what officers of the LAW have become as ones who must fulfill (corrupted) orders whether they believe in them or not. In a dog's world it is eat or be eaten and many have paid a high price mentally and emotionally for playing the game; like soldiers, these men and women require our empathy and support to reclaim the soul fragments they lost by causing harm, loss or committing fraud against fellow men and women their conscience holds guilt for until the negative charge of their actions can be healed and reintegrated.

This man told me to attend my hearing "with a loser's attitude" and apologize for being misguided, and then take whatever punishment they were willing to give me because otherwise they would be labelling me an 'Organized Pseudo-legal Commercial Argument (OPCA) Litigant' who wouldn't be listened to in the court anyway, he claimed.

As one who'd grown up believing myself to be a loser due to my lack of social status, I could have played the part quite easily but it went against every grain in my body. I called my law man, partly freaking out and questioning all that we had already done because I legitimately didn't know who to trust at that point. He was a 'no name' because he'd worked privately without the public accolades for years and liked it that way, and this other man had a website others were following which gave him the appearance of greater legitimacy.

Fortunately, my gut said going in with a "loser's attitude" was not in my best interest, especially because of what I'd experienced as a prisoner of the Mental Health Act already which I was reminded would be used against me as 'evidence' of my insanity. But even still that man gave me a key without necessarily intending to.

My law man had encountered the 'Meads v Meads' case law precedent from 2012 when the man acting as Judge tried to defame and discredit any man or woman using a common law or 'freeman of the land' argument by calling them 'vexatious litigants' that have no standing in a court of multiple jurisdictions. Dennis Meads, against who this precedent was set, must not have known how to contest this ruling, which has many holes in it, and so it has been used against others who have tried to be themselves without fully comprehending the dangers of the legal fiction and all the hidden joinders used to confuse and cause man to lose.

Joinder: the action of bringing parties together; union (of two unequal things).

And so it was that I learned how this case law precedent could be used against me and was able to protect myself ahead of time in my lawful notices.

The man acting as prosecutor did try this method at that first hearing I did not attend which another on the roster informed me of thereafter. The status didn't stick because my lawful claim protected me from their gaining jurisdiction over me that way but to those listening in on court that day it seemed my way hadn't worked which I believe to be part of an evil playbook to discredit and defame anyone who might expose the truth liars are paid to protect, defend and uphold.

While my situation may seem to be isolated, I believe we are living in a house of mirrors and the experience I could have had were it not for the Divine assistance and training I received, along with my own willingness to try something no one else I'm aware of was doing, is very relevant to the masses because given the corruption already obviously at play how long does it take before the 'Mental Health Act' becomes the 'Health Act' unless we intervene now?

My concern for all the men and women who had or were following David Robinson's five step notice process that require swearing an oath to the barons who evoked Article 61 is how that meets the 'OPCA Litigant' status requirement of having a guru, not to mention the volume of paperwork would seem vexatious (causing annoyance, frustration or worry) indeed.

The same can be said of any groups with an alternative approach or perspective of life, including all those brave men and women who have followed various freedom movements and used 'Notice of Liability' templates to protect themselves from the experimental injections or mask mandates that have been proven to cause more harm than good. Any references to 'evidence' without access to the source of the claim is deemed hearsay, no matter how legitimate, and thus deemed inadmissible in a court of LAW.

A template is not original so an ab-original status can be applied to the one trying a 'tried and tested' method; re-member, no status can stand on its own, it can only pose in public whereas a man or woman stands in private or public depending on how we wish to conduct ourselves as the instruments the Grand Orchestra Director (GOD) works through, so long as we are willing to claim the right to do as we wish (without causing harm, loss or fraud) and are then willing to stand on our claims in a court of competent jurisdiction under the supreme law.

The BIBLE may be an example of a script-u-re that has an authorized version available in the current-lie perverted courts of LAW to swear on but that's be-cause 'the crown' isn't actually worn by the woman acting as Queen at all. We all have a crown chakra that when activated is called a 'corona' which is the golden halo seen around the heads of enlightened ones we can all be if we dare to do the INNER work while also taking a stand for what is right, under the protection of the Divine's might.

High ranking members of the Masonic Order, Hollywood, banking industry, legal profession and religious orders know this but in order to gain entry into high-levels of society 'secrecy' is part of the deal.

Breaking rank or sharing hidden truths is dangerous in this world which is why 'truth tellers' have fallen under the archetype of 'whistle blowers' who speak out despite the high cost. I remember hearing John C. Maxwell say there is always a price to pay it's just a matter of when; pay upfront and enjoy the interest, play upfront and pay the interest.

What many have overlooked is the fact that our soul and the future of those yet to come here, through us, are what is currently on the line.

The Hierarchy Of Creation With Pirates At The Helm

14

We are spiritual beings having a human experience but have been conditioned to see ourselves as human beings seeking a spiritual experience.

What we were not made aware of is the fact hue-man reflects only one aspect of the man and is thus a creation by a creation other than the one source that created us all.

I first saw the Hierarchy of Creation on a "A Warrior Calls" meeting that I tuned into the day after my person was summoned for "Individual Failure to Comply" with the "Reopening Ontario Act" 2020 section 10(1). It was a joke I didn't find funny and feel the script writers will pay for selling out their fellow man because I believe we can and are now coming to inner-stand the stakes of this game and why we've been used as pawns in the 'mixed war' between the public and private that is currently at play.

Imagine a pyramid with 'energy' on the top to represent the creator or source of all. Regardless of the word (box) you put this creative source into, that is at the peak of it all.

Under energy is man-i-festation (man) and 'will of manifestation (woman)' which is what we are. Creators made in the image of the one we came from and return to but often feel separate from while here given all the boxes re-legions have called us to side with so that we don't focus on our similarities; instead religion has taught us to focus on our differences and hate those who threaten our BS by believing in something other than we do.

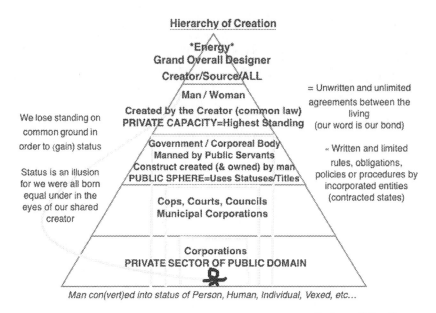

Hierarchy of Creation

Energy
Grand Overall Designer
Creator/Source/ALL

Man / Woman
Created by the Creator (common law)
PRIVATE CAPACITY=Highest Standing

Government / Corporeal Body
Manned by Public Servants
Construct created (& owned) by man
PUBLIC SPHERE=Uses Statuses/Titles

Cops, Courts, Councils
Municipal Corporations

Corporations
PRIVATE SECTOR OF PUBLIC DOMAIN

We lose standing on common ground in order to (gain) status

Status is an illusion for we were all born equal under in the eyes of our shared creator

= Unwritten and unlimited agreements between the living (our word is our bond)

= Written and limited rules, obligations, policies or procedures by incorporated entities (contracted states)

Man con(vert)ed into status of Person, Human, Individual, Vexed, etc...

By: Laura JE Hamilton

The Hierarchy of Creation.

Under man and woman, which is what we'll all be called in thousands of years when they dig our bodies up (if we haven't learned to trump the death cult by then, which is possible with practice), that's where we find the corporeal body known as 'government' which was designed to make life better for us. It's just that the de jure government which was created by the people, of the people, for the people became a 'de facto government' that imposed its rule on the very people who forgot it was created to serve us; hence government employees being called 'public servants' who are required, by law, to fulfill their public duties.

Cops, courts and councils were then created to uphold the legislation of the governments above them, within local municipalities, and then below these corporate entities we enter into the private sector of the public domain where private corporations come into the frame.

What we seem to have forgotten in the lead-up to the tyranny currently in effect is that everything under man/woman in the hierarchy are creations of man or woman and what I experienced firsthand when I got locked up, and then summoned for an alleged crime that has no victim (which means there was no crime), is that everything within the public domain is based on a legal fiction that converts us into something other than what we truly are (an original).

This is the difference between standing in the light and truth of who and whose we are versus taking on a status in the public that lowers our standing by converting us into the status, title or personage we are then said to be. And as we're starting to see, with each 'wave' of this Pendemic, which was written by men and women who believed themselves covered by anonymity and corporate liability protection, it will become more dangerous to accept the REALITY con-sent and acquiescence leads us to. *'Pirates of the Caribbean'* brought the term 'acquiesce' to my attention in a befitting line by the villainous 'captain' who said "I'm disinclined to acquiesce your request... means no" which is the point I believe we must now get to with the legalized pirates who have overtaken our courts, governments, corp-orations and households by playing 'creator' in a devious and undercover way.

Now it is time for us to see how we've been overtaken by pirates in professional (uni)forms who carry a box of flags (brands, logos, banners) to prey on the energy of people willing to invest energy to derive a sense of identity from them.

Our cultural obsession with social media is a prime example of how we have been trained to create profiles in the public domain that share private information and serve as an interface for us to engage with others using the same services. A Facebook, LinkedIn, Instagram, Twitter, YouTube or Telegram account give us access to these platforms where we present ourselves as we wish others to see us and engage with others in a virtual reality that feels very real when we're in it, yet over time the lines have got blurred and these profiles have come to mean a lot to us; how perfect with the increased censorship now upon us as a way to keep people in line who don't wish to lose access to accounts they've invested so much into building?

Here's where the mixed war between the public and private applies in the context of social media accounts and government created identities alike. We get to use both user accounts and government issued ID as a way to track our activities (consumption choices) in a public context and the more familiar we get with the concept the more second nature it becomes to share private information in the public domain without reserving our rights to it. So while our contributions to these entities (pictures, videos, posts, comments, likes and shares) may have originally been private information, once entered into the public domain ownership can be transferred or Intellectual Property (IP) stolen by others with limited protection for the creator of it.

In the context of the government who converts man/woman into statuses that limit our rights in accordance to rules implied to be accepted by participation in that domain, just like with our social media accounts, we will be implied to be surety for these accounts unless we recognize that the statuses we are implied to be are the equivalent of social media accounts that only reflect us but are not actually who we are. We know we are not our Facebook account yet the status of a 'person' is the equivalent in the context of the government.

The creator has rights to the creation but the creation does not have the same rights to the creator of it; unless a superior claim is made by another man or woman (not a suit acting on be-half of a corps) by way of lawful notice, a man or woman's claim stands as true and the man or woman can stand on that claim should further action be required within a court of competent jurisdiction (common law).

User accounts are meant to serve as an inter-face for services, similar to how the government uses our person (trust) to inter-act with the man or woman it was created in the name of; until we claim the right not to consent to being confused with our person, nor do we agree to be surety for it when no crime (harm, loss, fraud) has been committed, then we can be made liable for something that was created to serve us.

Surety: a person who accepts legal responsibility for another's debt or behavior.

Legal and lawful are not the same though in the eyes of the LAW they are implied to be.

Where the hierarchy is concerned, this means that man has rights to the government but the government does not have rights to man. It is for this reason that the government have created persons, titles and statuses that get applied to man to convert him into a creation the govern-mental body created and thus has rights to. See how it works?

Had I not been warned of the 'OPCA Litigant' status application it could have been used against me in the perverse court of LAW that no longer has man or woman's best interest at heart. So, once again, I am grateful to the man who offered me poor add-vice when informing me of a trap that had caught many along the path I'd been led to walk on my own two feet with the ability to feel my way through the darkness.

Trust is a huge part of that walk, so much so that one of the definitions of person is a 'trust' for the script writers have been very clever in setting traps for those too trusting of authority they have derived their identity from. Which is why I've learned to see authority as the 'author-i-tied my identity to' and no longer do, having learned who and whose I am as one willing to stand alone until others are willing to stand too and we truly become all one as we were all-ways meant to do.

Dates With Differing Intentions & Corrupted Reasons To Begin

15

When I set out to write this book it was for the wrong reasons.

I'd flown to California for what I thought was a professional connection and turned out to be a spontaneous six-day first date that I shut down the possibilities of shortly after my arrival; he was seeing someone else while going through a divorce at the time which was drama I wasn't interested in getting myself involved with. I had accepted the invitation because I felt he and I were meant to do business together and he was speaking at a conference in Phoenix that I thought could be a good networking opportunity as well. We were both dialled into WIIFM (What's In It For Me).

After a night on his sailboat hearing the 'inside scoop' on his inner circle that I'd met a few members of at the event I'd spoke at weeks earlier in Tampa, he told me that he'd booked a suite at the Venetian in Vegas for the next night, before finding out our intentions were not shared. He went to see his kids while I walked to a beach near the harbour where his boat was berthed and just as I sat down he called to say he was leaving for Vegas shortly and I could join him or stay on the boat and find a way to the airport on my own. As you can imagine, I opted to join him and got to face several patterns I'd hoped had died and been buried in the past.

What I've since learned is that our past patterns will always follow us if we don't change our relationship to and with them but I hadn't fully embodied or lived the theories I was playing with back then yet. So I got to learn this lesson the hard way.

We arrived in Vegas after several hours in the car, went to dinner at a place he loved while my appetite stayed home and after an awkward but civil night sticking to our respective sides of the King bed in our suite I could feel all my unresolved insecurities surfacing from the years I'd spent as a supported housewife without the title or a successful venture of my own. We were both trying to make the most of an awkward situation and after he took care of some business from our suite that morning, which triggered more memories of tip toeing around so as to not intrude on the breadwinner's important business, we hit the road for Phoenix.

Because I wasn't going to be his arm candy at the event, I no longer had a free ticket or room to share so I booked a room of my own in town and planned to hitch a ride with him back to Orange County for my flight after his event. While we drove from Vegas to Phoenix the next day however another hidden pattern arose that I was already carrying unspoken shame around from the first event where we'd met.

This was a new circle for me and I'd just parted ways with the JMT where so much of my identity had been vested for seven years at that point. I knew the power of networking and connecting with 'powerful players of the game' but what I hadn't expected was to be played in the process.

At the event where we'd met weeks before, one of his joint venture partners had invited me to an early morning workout and breakfast offsite which admittedly made me feel special. He'd 'picked me out' and wanted to get to know me, offering me a chance to fly directly to California to help him 'close the room' for a real estate deal.

My sister in law was checking in on my beloved cat, Julius Romeo, while I was away for the third trip in less than two months so I declined in the name of getting back as scheduled. When he then offered me another sales role doing something else, I didn't feel it so declined that offer too. I'd just got out of sales and wanted to 'strike out on my own' as a coach and Soul Realignment Practitioner, feeling more equipped to do so than my WEB of self-belief allowed. And so it was that he sold my own dream to me instead and an allegedly 'fast track' ticket to it.

He had a 'humanitarian trip' for speakers scheduled in New Zealand a few weeks later and made me a 'special offer' that he catered around everything I'd shared I was looking for at that transitionary time in my life; with the extensive sales training I'd received over the years I recognized a skilled salesman was working me but I wanted to have found my new tribe and knew I'd have to pay to play so overlooked my intuitive nudges to keep my wallet closed.

He'd pitched the opportunity in the conference the day before, alongside many other pitches, but the one on one time gave him insights to personalize 'the deal' and paint a picture I wanted to fit into. With nothing else lined up for when I returned, I let my ego make the decision and paid a high price for it.

We got back and I called my bank to raise my credit limit to make it possible. I signed the commitment form and he was gone, heading to California for the deal I could have joined him on. I felt proud of myself but also unsettled given his fast departure and all the other better suited offers being made at that event; suddenly I felt trapped.

I talked to the man hosting the event who was surprised but congratulatory of my decision to invest in myself. I then talked to another whose body language spoke volumes and his "look behind the curtain" warning had my alarm bells blaring before lunchtime. My pride quickly turned to shame and horror at what I had done and after another candid conversation with the host that helped me see I wasn't ready to truly make the most of that opportunity, I called my credit card company to cancel the charge and let the man know. He lost the $10k investment and I kept my money but lost even more in self-esteem, self-belief and self-worth.

When the host had invited me to California weeks later I was still recovering from the shame and humiliation I felt from that experience. Because I knew he would have received part of the money from that deal and he'd still been honest with me that I probably should get out of it if I could, I thought I could trust him to have my best interest at heart. I felt bad that he'd lost out on that money and then paid for my flight to California which I'd accepted despite knowing I just wanted to know who I was dealing with on a professional level which felt usery in a way I didn't like.

All of these factors made me vulnerable yet he'd shared a lot of great information at the first event and had published several books so I unconsciously respected him more than I did myself. On Maslow's Hierarchy of Motivational Needs, I was operating from the level of belonging while aiming for self-actualization. Self-respect was the step I kept tripping on.

During our drive he asked me questions about my desire to be a renowned coach, speaker and teacher like Louise Hay, Wayne Dyer and Marianne Williamson who I looked up to and the more I talked about my lack of clarity as to how I was going to get there he suggested a book was the best way forward. Paul Martinelli had suggested the opposite in the years I'd been on his Mentorship calls but in breaking away from that community, and trying to get into this one, I let him prove his point.

I'd started writing a book several times while living in England and had always felt called to get published so this man's suggestion resonated at a deep level. My dream was to get published with Hay House but I didn't know how to go about it and hadn't made the calls to find out, so when he 'happened' to have a publishing company and team that could pull it all together for me I reluctantly gave in. Wanting him to be right was another unresolved pattern I hadn't fully become conscious of yet.

He called an impromptu phone conference with his team to arrange a photoshoot for the cover in California the day before my scheduled flight and even though I'd told him the first package I'd pulled out of was a stretch and I didn't have anything else lined up yet, he added $5k to his offer evidently not caring if it bankrupted me or not.

My humiliation from the first deal was compounded by the fact his team were now involved in a decision I wasn't sure about and we hadn't even stopped driving. It was a bad situation and once again I felt trapped by the pressure to please.

When he dropped me off at the hotel I'd booked online before we left Vegas, I couldn't believe I'd just agreed to overcommit myself again with the same people. I called my Dad and he reaffirmed what I already knew, told me to cancel the deal and get myself home before getting back in the car with a man he equated to a snake salesman. This time I listened, pulled out before any money had been exchanged and rescheduled my flight from Phoenix feeling even more shame and guilt than I had weeks before. My WEB had been severely damaged but on the outside "I was fine" because my shame did not want anyone finding out about this change of mind too.

I was creating my own nightmare and the humiliation made my inner victim really scared but I was covering it well on the social media platforms where so much of my identity was derived at that time. I was trying to add value without clarity as to how I could best contribute to the world and I started a slow spiral down emotionally.

Proving myself to others was a pattern I hadn't realized had power over me and so it was that 'the book' began to unravel my self-image so that I could gain lived experience with all the theories I felt could help others transform their lives in the way I had yet to do for myself.

Homeless Heroes & Lost Till Found In Nevada

16

A couple months after this I tried to get close to the metaphoric fire again, this time with the other expert who'd gained my trust and respect by being willing to help me prepare for the speaking engagement that would have been part of that humanitarian trip if I hadn't been able to get out of it. That meant a lot to me.

I signed myself and my web designer lover up to attend his three-day conference for speakers in Las Vegas and we visited the Grand Canyon for his birthday afterwards which was memorable for several unexpected reasons.

The conference itself was good and I found myself over-contributing because I was bursting to share all the tips and tricks I'd learned from all the years I'd already spent in the personal growth and leadership sphere. It was valuable information but not necessarily valued input because I was just another participant being offered a spot in yet another high-end coaching program. No judgement, it's just the nature of the industry.

On the first or second night of the conference my friend and I had a lover's dispute while walking the strip and he went one way and I the other. To stay safe as a woman on my own I teamed up with others walking the same way as I returned to our room and got to sprinkle magic along my path in the process. Shortly after I'd got back, he came in to grab the marijuana and pipe we'd got on our first day there and told me he'd met some guys with a limo he was going to party with in the black pyramid. He didn't invite me which I was partly glad for, given I was paying for the trip and wanted to be on the ball the next day, but not getting included hurt too; a common pattern I'm still clearing up five years later.

After a restless night alone, I got up early to journal and when he came in to crash early the next morning I grabbed the weed and left to get grounded outdoors.

We were staying in the Westin Hotel which is at the far end of the infamous strip and it was still so early that traffic was still quiet. I walked to the rock bed in the corner of the back parking lot and settled in to smoke and journal.

One of the arguments my friend and I had been having was how often I compliment strangers in passing which he felt took away from being present with him. So when I saw two people cross the side road next to where I was sitting, I suspected they were homeless but genuinely wanted to compliment the woman on her hair. I held back because of the criticism I'd received and went back to journaling. Suddenly I heard a man's voice shout "Do you have water?"

I did have water but didn't want to give it to him so tried to shrink into my journal when suddenly I heard a Gatorade bottle filled with water slamming down next to me. He'd asked to see if I was in need and I'd expected the worst. I could have politely thrown it out on my way back into the hotel as I wasn't going to drink it but figured someone else could benefit from it so I called him back just as his lady friend returned.

They came over to get the bottle and I offered them my packed pipe as a peace offering which they came around the low cement blocked wall to join me for. We started talking as we sat together and Linda suddenly got really honest. The man silently took his leave without saying a word and there Linda and I sat together for nearly two hours as I held space for her to release pent up emotions after more than twenty years as an abused woman.

She told me that her partner had put her in hospital several times, on the brink of death, but months before he'd died and she'd become homeless. Without her abuser she didn't know who she was and the night before, in a state of desperation, she'd prayed for a miracle.

When I showed up and genuinely cared to hear her story, she felt I was the answer to her call and as a result she trusted me and my input.

As she told me her story and moved her emotions, she stomped her feet and hit her hands on the ground, screaming at times, like a grown toddler having a temper tantrum, and I held space for her to unfold without interference or judgement. It was sacred work we were doing together and it was here I learned that we are all homeless until we come home to ourselves.

Another invaluable lesson Linda gave me that day was when I shared my doubt about the story of Jesus and the buy-bull in general. I do believe the man existed but his name was not the same as the stories written about him for as I have come to believe Je su(i)s is an i and space shy of the French word for "I am" and as one who tried to guide people out of other people's BS I believe the man himself would roll in his grave to know his message had been misconstrued, though he knew it was bound to happen.

I was less certain of myself and that belief then and I'll always remember Linda looking me directly in the eyes begging me not to take Jesus away from her. For she had given me the respect she had not yet claimed for herself and knew that I could rock her world in a devastating way if I said he was not the saviour she needed him to be.

I don't remember exactly what I said now but do remember seeing how much power she had given me in that short time and I told her to keep him for as long as it empowered her to do so for I did not wish to take away the foundation of her belief system without being able to support her in the rebuilding of it. I didn't even know where I stood where his story was concerned specifically but the last thing I wanted was to cause more harm than good.

Whatever happened to Linda after that fateful exchange I know not but she greatly impacted my life and I have wished her well ever since. If only I had seen the pattern she was reflecting for me back then, it could have saved me a great deal of pain, I say at 3:33 on the clock.

All numbers have different meanings and are one of the ways we are able to receive messages from the Divine. According to one online source, the number 333 is said to show that your guardian angel is beside you to provide you with the strength and ability to take one step at a time. It could be a sign that joy can exist even in the worst situations and given the pattern I was acknowledging in the moment I saw the clock, I feel it may be significant for you to be aware of the symbolic significance of numbers so you can notice synchronicities when they cross your path. Pay attention to repeating numbers that show up in your reality for the Universe speaks to us through signs, symbols, omens and patterns, whether you believe me or not.

In addition to what my experience with Linda taught me, my travel companion's error at the beginning of our trip also taught me a lot about myself and sticking together.

Somehow, he managed to forget his passport in the backseat pocket of our flight to Vegas and one of the air stewards let him know using Facebook messenger; he discovered the message the last day of the conference and was still waiting for a reply when we picked up our rental and left for the Grand Canyon.

The man was kind enough to offer to ship it to us but we didn't have a home base for him to even send it to given I hadn't booked anything after our mule ride into the Canyon so we had more flexibility for our final two days. It was a stressful situation!

Amazingly we stayed high vibing despite the situation and got upgraded to a black Mustang because of how much fun we were having with other customers while waiting in line and so our road trip had an added element of power and beauty.

The mule ride was an interesting experience and my friend did an amazing job staying present despite the uncertainty of his situation. But after our Canyon experience as we drove through the Nevada desert en route back to Vegas things got real.

Along the way we came to a place called Mesquite where a dispensary with a hummingbird logo was located and a hotel was advertised for $25 per night. We decided to call that home while he made arrangements to get his passport shipped to him and I figured out what I was going to do as the sponsor of our trip.

I'll always remember the 'decision point moment' shortly after we parked and were getting our things from the car when, in my frustration at the situation, I told him he'd better figure it out quickly. He said "please don't give up on me already" and I saw the two possible timelines that stemmed from that moment.

One saw us drive back to Vegas the next day to return the rental on time, find him a place to stay in wait for his passport to be shipped back while I flew back home feeling horrible having left a friend in need who would have resented me forever after. He said he'd have understood but the trust between us would have been eroded to an irreparable level from my perspective if the tables were turned. The other timeline involved more effort and expense on my end but I would know I'd done my best and could live with that better. I wouldn't want to be abandoned if in a similar situation so chose the second timeline.

I called the airline to report the situation and had to pay $66 each to move our flights to later in the week, leaving enough time for the passport to be shipped to the hotel which was far less than I was expecting. The rental extension cost most and other things too but all these years later we're still friends and have been there for one another through some tough times; his family treat me like one of their own too which meant the world to me during the past few.

It also gave us time to integrate all that we'd experienced before returning home to 'face the music' and figure out how to monetize all the experiences our journey had gifted us with, even though no one else could see their value yet. Let me tell you from experience, that's not a comfortable place to be yet how can anyone see the vision we're meant to birth until we do it and then they marvel at our creation and how lucky we seem to be?

PEACEFULL INNER
Warriors United & Untied

17

That trip was one of many I took with the intention of getting 'the book' done while away but each time I stirred up so many energies and unintegrated aspects of myself I felt insecure and unsure how to help others while feeling like a mess in myself.

I also made a growth-infused error that first year writing it when I publicly announced I'd be having a book launch party to celebrate my thirtieth birthday without respecting the law of gender that says everything has its own natural gestation period; I hadn't dived deep enough inward to strengthen the foundation on which my outer kingdom would be based so in a way I believe I was protected from myself.

Moving into my grandparents' basement that year instead of branching out into the world as I'd intended felt like a failure, as did so many of my efforts in the years I've been here since. It wasn't easy for me to break the pattern of taking other people's projections personally, especially because I overshared with people who couldn't understand the vision I was still trying to piece together for myself. And I made the mistake of trusting people who cared more about what they could get from me than they ever did for me. All of it took time to grow and heal from but I am stronger for having gone through it and grateful for all the teachers who came into my life for a reason, season or lifetime to help me learn the power of discernment.

In strengthening my porous boundaries, I finally stopped confiding in people who didn't want to go where I was heading nor did they believe I would ever get there, or even want me to. I also stopped leaking energy into the vacuous space of the virtual reality platforms so much of my identity had been vested in for so many years, and I finally stopped pouring energy into people and things that took more than they gave back. I'd given certain people a vote within my INNER Kingdom and got knocked down countless times when their criticism and condemnation cut me to the core, slashing my self-esteem account and breaking my heart in the process.

Years before getting to this point, when the con video game kicked off in March 2020, my self-image was at yet another reset point. I was afraid that what I'd experienced and heard while in the belly of the beast was now being rolled out publicly and without intending to I drove wedges between myself and loved ones whose cognitive dissonance couldn't allow what I shared to be true, nor did all I was worried about come to pass as fast as I'd feared it might. Their worlds had not been impacted the way mine had and they were content with the lives they felt they were leading whereas I was horrified by all the corruption so many seemed content enough to turn a blind eye to.

The "it's always been that way" excuse didn't seem good enough to me and I was doing my best to call for personal responsibility and liability in a system I could see was designed to convert people into patients and dependents as had been tried with me. In many ways I had resisted this fate and over time managed to rise above it mentally, emotionally, and spiritually but my literal reality seemed underwhelming to those who couldn't see what I was building behind the scenes and my wounded warrior heart was guarded and on the defensive.

My beloved cat's final gift to me was the reminder of life's sacred nature and so it is that in the month since his passing I've pulled my energy back from all the places and people I'd given it to so freely. I intentionally took charge of my life by cleaning up my act so I no longer leak energy as carelessly as I did before which is how you now hold that which took so much of my Time, Energy, Effort, Attention, and Money to finally package in a useful way.

I've stopped running from the unpleasant emotions that go with not having status in a world based in fiction and I've stopped needing acceptance from people who don't know how to accept themselves let alone someone who sees the world so differently from the way it's presented to be. I've settled into myself deeper than ever before and am facing the feel(ing)s as they show up without judging myself in the process. Or at least am doing my best to without the coping mechanism that drained so much of my energy for so many years (weed).

Every journey begins with a first step from precisely where we are and after sitting in judgement of myself, and those who didn't get me for longer than I'd like to admit, I'm finally ready to share what it means to be a PEACEFULL INNER Warrior United and Untied from the not-nows that need no longer steal our power.

PEACEFULL is an acronym which means each letter has its own meaning:

> **Passion** is the spark of light dancing in our hearts that shine through eyes willing to face the lies of what was previously oblivious and now made obvious because we stopped fearing the unknown. Passion is an object of someone's love, liking, or desire and is said to be connected to "the suffering and death of Jesus" which I see to be the "I am" in me that calls me to life, as it does you too. Passion is hard to control and is often activated in our relationships with another. Passionate love is intense and can be blinding which Bruce Lipton refers to as 'the honeymoon effect' in a book by the same title which implies our dysfunctions compensate for the other for a time but unless we deal with our feels they'll resurface with a passionate vengeance.

> **Enthusiasm** is an intense feeling of excitement we can either express outwardly or enjoy within ourselves behind a smile that gets others curious. It bubbles up from the heart when we look forward to something

we anticipate will benefit us or others and gives us a sense of significance.

Authenticity is rare in today's fictitious reality but it's time for us to take the masks and personas off so that we can be our true and full selves without reservation. Authenticity is based in truth and living in alignment with higher ideals that help us lift the lid on our own self-image. It requires us to be honest with ourselves and others which can feel vulnerable but is worth it in the end when we come to know the only one we sleep with every night and wake up to start each new day with as winners of the 86,400 second lottery each day gifts us with.

Clarity is connected to the vision we hold of ourselves, the world and our place within it. It's about daring to see the literal world we live in, as well as the mythic, symbolic and energetic elements underlying the story that raises our perspective to a higher vantage point. True clarity comes from combining what we see and feel to create a vision we are willing to stand up for.

Encouragement is the experience of supporting one another outwardly without attachment to the outcome but it starts within where we must become our own cheerleader. And despite what we've been taught about selfishness and egoism, if you treat yourself as your number one and I do the same, and so does everyone else, where is the number two?

The answer is that there wouldn't be one because it is only when we put others before ourselves that we bring that energy into the equation. Hurting people hurt people because they feel inferior and need to steal power; healed people heal people because they are present in the moment where all power exists and can encourage others without comparison. That is power-full!

'Find your tribe' is the missing link for those who feel isolated and limited by the judgements and projections of others, especially in a cult-u-re as fake as the one we've current-lie got. The Realistic Evidence Appearing Legit In Tomorrow's Yesterday (REALITY) is that so few people actually like themselves that they will throw garbage into your INNER Kingdom if you'll let them just to make sure you continue running in circles where they can track with you. Kick out the polluters and toxic influences in your life to make space for something that will serve you better and release yourself from the guilt of putting distance between yourself and lower vibing individuals who need you to stay small in order to steal your power; when you are strong enough to be your authentic self and stand in your power, they can choose to raise the bar and join you, or not, but that's up to them. Join others willing to do the same in the name of being the change we seek in this world with PEACEFULL INNER Warriors United and Untied!

'Understand what is yours' is the way you can play with life even when others try to spray their limitations your way. Use this as your umbrella to filter external projections that don't belong to you, nor even necessarily originated with the one spraying them your way in the first place; few people knew how to use the umbrella of discernment when they got hit by the projections they took on. Tune into how things make you feel and ask yourself "is this mine?"

Listen for the answer that comes from within as your subconscious will respond with 'yes' or 'no' so you can then move to the next question: "can I let this go?"

Once you hear the reply ask "will I let this go?" and if not "why not?"

Start to track your stories and recognize how many of them were never yours in the first place.

Practice this simple four question process so that you can redirect your attention onto something that will serve you better than the BS others will try to infect you with and do your best to spend less time with those who drain your energy. Energy vampirism is very real and you can tell when you've been someone's meal by how you feel; get away, recharge and get your umbrella ready for next time as the higher you vibe the more you'll need it!

'**Love what arises**' because it's revealing itself to be healed whether you feel ready for it or not. Each emotion has its own personality because in the past we tended to suppress, repress, depress, compress or deny the energies in motion we didn't know how to handle. In the process we left behind an aspect of ourselves that has yet to receive the acceptance that we all crave so now it is time for us to stop 'taking a pill' to chill instead of be still with the part of us that's ready to be given a chance at life. It's time to do some INNER Kingdom excavating with full readiness to feel the discomfort of those aspects of our cells that are now ready to heal; re-member we must feel our way through the growing pains without trying to get comfortable in an uncomfortable process. Prepare to comfort yourself through the discomfort in functional ways by practicing full presence despite the pain, shame or blame of needing to reclaim lost aspects of yourself. What healing into wholeness you do heals you and many generations forward and backwards in your lineage too so dare to do the INNER work for all of you whether you are recognized or appreciated for it or not; people like the familiar patterns they know so don't take it personally if others don't like the changes you're making in your life!

'Let go of your attachments to the not-now' means releasing yourself from the crosses you have crucified yourself on along your path. In Clarissa Pinkola Estes' book *Women Who Run with the Wolves* she recommends a process called 'descansos' which is the process of reflecting on your life to pinpoint all the choice point moments when something in or about you died right there on that spot, where your journey was halted unexpectedly and you left a part of yourself behind. You can do a timeline with crosses to mark each spot that shaped you and irrevocably changed your life and the lives of others too which often leads to trauma bonding with those also left behind or who have shared a similar experience. Be care-full with these kinds of connections for they can't afford for you to heal without risking losing the trauma bond on which your relationship is based.

It is time to take your experiences to the quarry station where you can mine them for their lessons without having to carry the weight of the trauma with you any longer. And if the thought of letting go of what no longer serves you feels terrifying, dare to love the part of you that has been crushed underneath the debris of this memory ever since it happened, when you turned your back on yourself because you didn't know how else to cope. You are no longer alone for you now have access to tools you didn't before.

INNER is also an acronym for Individual Needs Necessitate Resonance, Resilience and Respect, not necessarily in that order though it is the way it came together for me.

Resonance is all about harmony and discord. From a 'law of attraction' perspective, it means 'like attracts like' in a Universe that does not differentiate negatives so where our focus goes our energy flows.

The Universe is eager to serve us from the Cosmic Kitchen of creation. We just have to get clear about what we want and use our contrast to help us gain clarity about what those undesirable circumstances or experiences helped us see we want instead of that. So instead of resenting negative or draining circumstances and situations, we can see them as opportunities to be more intentional in our creative process moving forward.

Resilience is about 'bouncing back' emotionally when life doesn't go the way we'd planned, or when things go even better than we'd expected and we need to get regrounded in a higher level reality than we used to have. We expect to need to 'bounce back' after a low but rarely do we consider the need to accommodate new highs; it's why so many lottery winners lose all the money they won and find themselves in debt on top of the winnings they burned through.

Learning to maneuver the 'Highrise of Emotional Awareness' helps to 'love what arises' and 'let go of attachments' to energies that are meant to be in motion so dare to care for your INNER health and well-being as much as you do your physical form. The healthier we are emotionally the easier it becomes to stay strong despite the storms of change that come to test our commitment to becoming whole at the soul level.

Respect is directly tied to a healthy self-esteem because we set a high value on that which we respect or admire but rarely are we taught to genuinely respect ourselves instead of the worldly attributes of status, title and fame we're awarded for how we play the game of life. This relates to the story of a house built on sand that will cave under pressure from the elements compared to the house built on solid ground. External 'trappings of success' are like the house on sand that has no-thing to stand on when the winds of change blow away the foundation we didn't take time to thoroughly secure before building.

INNER work is solid because it cannot be stripped away despite the chaos of the world we live in, especially where the currency we currently place so much importance on is determined by authority who also benefit from the trust we've been raised to believe we must place outside of ourselves. If the concept of 'fiat currency' is new to thee, you will see how everything we've been taught had worth and value has not been what it seems. My fear has been how many will fall when the old system crumbles and all that's been deemed valuable no longer carries any weight; rebuilding community connections is part of a strong foundation for civilizations and now is our time to create a better future with the ones who will live it and who came here with keys and insights we have yet to find because we thought the holders of them too younge to be part of the process. That's BS. Growing up is not tied to a number and those in younge bodies possess great wisdom it is our responsibility to hold space for them to feel safe enough to bring forward and put into practice.

With eyes to see the lies we've been sold for generations, including the karmic repercussions of acting against our Divine nature in the name of fulfilling orders we are paid to complete, we must seriously ask ourselves a sacred and significant question: what is the point of gaining the whole world while losing our soul in the process?

Wars are fought by men and women on behalf of man-made nations we identify with, believe ourselves to belong to and are willing to die to defend those within its borders because we love our people. Soldiers get paid to wear dog tags for the elites which I hate to say because it sounds judgemental of the ones wearing them, but do we judge pets wearing tags just because it shows who owns them? No, we feel for them, especially when their masters are cruel and unworthy of the positions of authority they hold.

Messengers have been killed for delivering controversial messages throughout history because so many are looking to be offended and have a reason to take out their rage and frustration on something they can steal (power) from. They take such messages personally without realizing the ally their person is not, as I have found with my own and dare to share in hopes we can begin to respect our cells and selves enough to stop accruing karma that isn't ours by causing harm, loss and fraud to our fellow man and woman who feel trapped in a corrupted system too.

Soldiers are duty-bound to fulfill orders they may or may not agree with, just as the public servants working for govern-mental bodies are required to do, and the corporate dogs who must bite when their boss tells them to; the HR personnel who also are accruing karma by creating policies and procedures that coerce employees to participate in an experiment of control, corruption and intentional chaos never thought they'd find themselves in this category but grocery store personnel didn't expect to become 'frontline workers' either, yet it happened.

That being said the 'warrior' is an archetype (familiar pattern) that gets filled in with energy that is either SCARED or SACRED, and we get to choose which side we will fill; the con vid game and corporate entities rely on us being scared so beware the switching of sides.

According to Caroline Myss' book *Sacred Contracts* which is all about archetypes, a warrior in his or her shadow (scared) side will sell their power on the open market, often with complete disregard for the buyer's cause, but when empowered (acting on the sacred side) knows what they will not sell out for regardless of the proposed reward. Soldiers and officers of the law are often forced into their scared side because they are not free to choose which orders they follow for their identity is directly tied to their position; knights are the same because they had to take a knee to be knighted and surrender their free will to fulfill the whims of the one they bowed down to. Corporate employees at all levels must do the same to hold their position.

When on the sacred side, this part of us can warn us when we are in danger of aligning our might with an unjust or purely self-interested cause but it's easy to flip into the scared side of this archetype when 'tipped off' internally without a safe place to turn as I experienced in 2019 and tried to call the embassy to say I was more significant than it seemed at the time; in case you ever feel like you've become a threat to the unseen forces that know how powerful you are in this game, don't try that. You'll find your whole country is supposed to be safe, but who else would be crazy enough to try what I did back then and be surprised by the result? I ask jokingly for yet again, "That is what you should not do, now let that be a lesson to you!"

I hadn't considered the shadow side of an archetype I've always had and assumed the warrior archetype is more common than has proved to be true. We often take our inherent strengths for granted and apply them to others without seeing the archetypes they have in place of the ones we project onto them because they're so active within us. Caroline says we share the four survival archetypes (victim, child, saboteur and prostitute) and then have eight that are unique to us; the warrior is one of mine and judging others for not having it only plays into the divide and conquer war strategy that's been implemented against us to keep us weak.

During my awakening I called out patterns I'd become aware of that hurt people I love and acted in ways I would regret if it helped but instead can only say I'm genuinely sorry to everyone I hurt in the process of outing dysfunctional patterns I'd become aware of without grace or compassion for the discomfort doing so caused others. When I then got put in a situation that only the Universe could have orchestrated, just as my shattered heart was starting to heal, my beloved Grandma who'd always been my best friend and confidant, got stuck in quarantine for her final months alive without understanding why the family she'd devoted her life to said we couldn't come to see her due to hospital protocols. It was devastating and without her to call for peace and civility we fractured just as the con video game program intended, or at least that was my experience of it.

My warrior heart built up a wall that kept everyone except my Papa at a distance as he had remained faithful to me when I felt others had not been, and they felt the same about me; people will forget what you said, they'll forget what you did but they'll never forget how you made them feel and there's been a lot of hurt on both sides through all of this that now needs openness and compassion to heal if willingness is present. In marketing there's a saying "some will, some won't, who cares, next!?" and while that's reality in business we must remember that we are the players on the field so making peace with one another by owning our part in damaged dynamics goes a long way in the bigger picture where we all count and matter.

I channeled my pain into building new community connections by trying to find others who saw the corruption as I did and were willing to do something about it but found myself giving up on the 'blue pillers' just as the evil had counted on. And while my realization came late I believe we choose our fate and it's time to shift the hate we've let grow between one another for I believe this has been a common experience through this con game where shame and blame are tools to remain safely separate, behind heart walls we deny we have up.

DENIAL: Didn't Even kNow I Am Lying.

I see this pattern in many of the 'freedom fighters' who have become isolated from loved ones in the name of sharing an ugly truth that isn't safe enough for FEAR-FULL people to accept without a better solution for them to turn to. Warriors are used to fighting for what we believe in and there are many who will lash back to protect and defend what they know to keep themselves feeling safe but we cannot win this war by abandoning one another for it is our souls that are on the line and doing so means we are covertly helping the evil win.

There is no running from this because we are the ones driving the planes dropping bombs and chemtrails that change the weather patterns and poison the common lands we came here to leave better for our having lived.

We are the ones who will be faced with an order that takes a life we are liable for the loss of when our soul leaves and re-counts all we did while here so let's steer clear of accruing karma on be-half of a corps(e) that needs us to think we are less significant than we are.

Resistance, Resentment and Revenge are the dysfunctional R's that lead us into our scared side where Regret is generally the reward and pride tends to keep us from fully feeling the pain of this dysfunctional dynamic until it's too late. Let's not wait to find compounded passion (compassion) for one another during this scary time in our shared story. Love is the solution that fear needs us to forget so may we re-member we are all in this together.

My hope is that these words can inspire some of those working for the devil (lived backwards) to step into their sacred side of the archetypes within; not everyone has a warrior archetype within them as has been made clear within the collective during the early stages of this war of terrorism we are called to untie our identities from, but we all share the victim, child, prostitute and saboteur who become guardians in their sacred sides.

For too long the public cry has been for the 'war on terrorism' by strategists who knew this would only grow the very focus of these efforts: war and terror. The law of non-resistance says what we resist persists so may we shift our focus and bring love back into the frame.

As many have discovered pushing back against the system has a high cost but not all is yet lost and we must do our part to start dealing with the war within between the scared and sacred sides of our own personalities.

United we stand, divided we fall. Scrambled we find united to be untied from the lies of the Ma Tricks the leaders of our homes didn't know they were telling. "Forgive them for they know not what they do" and choose to be the example that helps them change their ways.

By winning the war within we can begin to balance the scales of justice by recognizing how 'divide and conquer' has been the war strategy used to tear (nuclear) families apart in a war we weren't told we were in. Just like the farmer whose son's accident saved him from a war that wasn't his to fight we can only find our place when we are willing to hold our space with grace. Not because someone told us to or paid us to do it but because we saw the common hue of convenient enemies we were taught to hate, distrust and fear in the name of protecting ours and gaining theirs where possible. There are no winners when we become sinners because we followed orders that fragmented our souls and made us less whole.

Psychosis, The Crazy Ones, Choice Points & Survival Archetypes

18

The Sacred Sojourn of the Soul is a spiritual portrayal of the hero's journey by Joseph Campbell and while both begin at home, in the comfort zone of the known, we must take a step back to reflect on the journey of life that has brought us to the present moment and find the lessons it gifted us with so we no longer fall prey to people and circumstances we previously didn't know to beware of.

It's like the man walking along a sidewalk so 'up in his head' he fails to see the manhole along his path and falls in. The next day, bruised and battered from his fall, he walks the same way but this time crosses the street before having to meet the same fate he did before. That is how we grow from pain we know we don't wish to go through again and while it takes added effort to do things a different way initially, over time the new way will become second-nature as all familiar patterns do over time.

The only true failure in life is failing to learn from the experiences that cause us harm because we refused to mind the internal alarm our nervous system sends its messages to us through. Which was yet another lesson I learned when my sympathetic nervous system got stuck in the 'on' position without owning the fact I was ungrounded so the information I was trying to share couldn't land with those I was trying to connect with through it. I even recognized I was going too fast to make the information safe for people to receive because I sensed the disconnect yet I kept pushing because force was the pattern I'd used to work myself up to that point months before.

My cells were vibrating faster than usual because I was experiencing a naturally induced expanded state of awareness and lack of sleep meant my body was working overtime to find balance without support; sleep is when the body processes energies in motion and refreshes itself so by not making space for this basic need in the name of higher level needs I wasn't in a position to bring about (world peace was my mission and I was 'all in' without being fully in my own body) I couldn't help anyone including myself. I feel many leaders with a lot of passion go through something like this because our mission seems impossible to those committed to the way things are so to them we seem to have lost our minds and to compensate for their disbelief we push our agenda even harder; when I was going through this I recognized and openly said I'd fallen out of my head and fell squarely into my heart but the psychiatrists 'diagnosed' it as a psychotic episode or psychosis.

The National Alliance on Mental Illness characterizes 'psychosis "as disruptions to a person's thoughts and perceptions that make it difficult for them to recognize what is real and what isn't. These disruptions are often experienced as seeing, hearing and believing things that aren't real or having strange, persistent thoughts, behaviors and emotions." But the Mental Health system does not take into account the energetic nature of the world we live in that cannot be explained rationally by a 'ration of lies' that denies the supernatural elements of life.

I can appreciate how crazy my claims seemed for where I was then and the fact I was sharing information in pieces others couldn't put together as fast as I was expressing them, nor did I have the full picture the way I thought I did at the time, but until things got real and I lost the deciding vote over my own life, I was having too much fun to slow down. And while I returned to my naturally higher-vibing state days after my insane adventure began and I refused to let FEAR overtake me any longer than it already had, while also moderating my expression of joy more appropriately for the laboratory setting I was being observed within, I then had a lot of lived experience that didn't match the way I'd thought the world was beforehand which took time to unpack while I rebuilt my damaged INNER WEB and continued to face my own denials.

It's been a journey which starts and ends with joy and leaves an urne between which is a ballot box I was protecting better than the 2020 US election (…couldn't resist) in some ways but my survival archetypes were still transitioning into their sacred sides as I owned the label of crazy, taking solace in Jack Kerouac's poem:

"Here's to the crazy ones.
The misfits. The rebels. The troublemakers.
The round pegs in the square holes.
The ones who see things differently.
They're not fond of rules.
And they have no respect for the status quo.
While some may see them as the crazy ones, we see genius.
Because the people who are crazy enough to think they
can change the world, are the ones who do."

Packaging my BS in a form others can review in their own time offers a level of safety and comfort that is respect-full because a settled nervous system can receive information and work with it in a way that a triggered one cannot.

After I was released from that insane experience I discovered Stephen Porges' Polyvagal Theory that breaks down the connection between self and social awareness of communication from the perspective of the autonomic nervous system which is responsible for both the sympathetic and parasympathetic nervous systems. There are said to be three tracks within our system that influences whether we feel safe to connect with others, unsafe to connect which triggers our internal fight or flight mechanism, or when we shut down and let FEAR win. I'll always remember my fourth night in the system when I was terrified because I was trapped in a place I didn't know how to get out of and somehow hacked myself with an open and closed circuiting exercise I intuitively led myself through in the middle of the night that got me back on track and shifted my experience for the remainder of my imprisonment.

I placed my left hand on my heart, my right hand on my belly and touched the tip of my big toes together as I deeply inhaled and envisioned love, peace, faith and joy circulating through my system. On my exhale breath I separated my toes and removed my hands from my body as I imagined all False Emotion Appearing Real leaving my body, and then I repeated this exercise for as long as it took for me to feel more settled within myself and the situation I didn't know how to get myself out of. I remember pushing through the tiredness I felt given the lack of sleep I'd had leading up to this 'turning point' experience where I empowered myself to feel safe despite the dysfunctional situation I found myself in.

I also called on the reassuring experience I'd had in one of my DMT ceremonies when the pain and FEAR of all I was facing became too much for me to handle but I knew I'd chose it so needed to face it; I remember the comfort I experienced by repeatedly saying "It's OK. It's ok, it's okay" in different ways and tones until my own voice became comforting to me in the way I'd always looked to others to do for me. When I first heard Jane 'Nightbirde' Marczewski's song "It's OK" I remember crying at the gift her beautiful soul was able to give the world before she left before her thirty-second birthday which I'd celebrated as a prisoner during that insane experience.

Life is always happening in the moment yet we all have different capacities and abilities to process information for how it resonates for us and by trying to share alternative and ungrounded perspectives others couldn't receive it was draining, confusing and ineffective for all involved. But I learned from it and hope my sharing of this experience helps others do better than I did then when I didn't understand what was happening within me and others didn't either.

These experiences taught me a lot and while it took time to understand and integrate it helped me recognize that information is not the only dots we need to connect for it is us who are the lights of the world that need to stand together in formation, holding our own ground while taking into consideration those around us who feel our vibration before they can hear our words. Like the Canadian geese who take turns leading to cut the wind for the ones following behind and who are willing to fly point when the one leading needs to rest, as we all do at times, we must learn how to cooperate with others without trying to change them to make ourselves more comfortable.

The more light we embody the more shadow we expose and facing those aspects of ourselves at first can be disconcerting (causing one to feel unsettled) because it's unfamiliar so instead of judging and trying to force one another into less emotionally charged states through suppression, repression, depression or denial, why not train ourselves to hold space for the organic unfoldment of souls in hue-man form?

Titles and statuses don't give people a break because they make us cogs in a machine that requires we either get the job done or we get replaced. From a technocratic perspective this works but from a creative perspective it's unsustainable and leads to burn out, mental health problems and emotional dysfunction.

It is no coincidence the DSM5-4-3-2-1's creation is directly tied to the profitability of diagnosing mental health dis-orders which is where we must real-eyes (realize) the fact you cannot clean a messy room by just throwing cleaning products on it or paying someone to fix us, like a machine. We're not broken, we just sometimes go through dis-regulated states and need support from within, and on the outside, to get back on track.

People suffering from 'mental problems' need help facing the energies in motion (emotion) showing up in the moment with compounded tension from past moments where FEAR suppressed, repressed, depressed, compressed or denied uncomfortable feelings and created scary stories about them to re-mind us how to feel about those emotions the next time they re-emerged.

While we've been trained to think that's what the professionals are supposed to help with, theoretical add-vice can only help to the point where rubber meets the road and the one who gained access to the tools has to use them which is the hard part. Programming offered to shift thought patterns may be well intended but cleaning up a trap from the inside means the trap is where one stays; the question just becomes how long will it take until the next 'episode' and what damage will the trapped one do to themselves and others then (and in the lead up to it).

Disordered thinking requires unpacking the emotions driving the chaos within and offering quick fix solutions to suppress the uncomfortable emotions showing up to be healed (through drugs or electric shock therapy which is a commonly prescribed treatment still) only keeps scared people in the driver's seat of their own lives hoping a passenger will keep them on track and the damage some passengers do is worse than the dysfunctional behaviours in the first place. It's truly insane which by Einstein's definition means doing the same thing while expecting different results.

No one has it all together or fully figured out, even if they do a great job pretending they do, and I feel that our youth especially need to be let in on that secret.

Secrets are destructive to the soul because they require sacrificing the truth for the sake of keeping a lie quiet and those willing to speak out often get called snitches that need stitches and sometimes wind up in ditches. But if not now then when will be a better time to do what has not yet been done which is to bring the sacred back in place of the secrets so many have compromised their souls to uphold?

The Lion King is a famous Disney movie about the 'circle of life' but have you ever considered how the lie-on roars to defend his pride while the true king of the jungle roars with the power of his ancestors backing him just as I am now? Not because I am a king specifically but be-cause I know who and whose I am and stand under the power of the spoken word when used with (con)viction.

Viction: an inclination to undertake a certain kind of work, often in response to a perceived summons; a calling.

Conviction: a firmly held belief or opinion, or, a formal declaration that someone is guilty of a criminal offense, made by the verdict of a jury or the decision of a judge in a court of law.

Our words hold power which is why we spell them out when we write to right wrongs we are pressured to uphold for the sake of 'saving face' (to avoid having other people lose respect for oneself) at the expense of our self-respect. I dare say the cost is too high and the lies need be exposed now by those willing to pay the price lest our souls pay the ultimate price in the end when we are called to account for the life we led while we lived and got to be the example of love incarnate who inspired others to be true to their authentic nature too.

Accountability: the fact or condition of being accountable for results; responsibility.

We have become disconnected from what truly matters in life in the name of defending Belief Systems backed by nothing but our trust and when the markets crash during the anticipated 'great reset' and people lose their identities that have been fully vested in a corporate world, based on illusions, we need to be there for one another or we will be systematically taken out by heartless drones we allowed to rule the roost.

Roost: a temporary place to rest or stay.

We all need to take a few steps back to ask what the point of achieving world-lie success is if we lose our connection to the people we came here to play (the game of life) with in the process of achieving it.

Meeting the internal leadership team we all share in common can help us better understand how we've been played and made to fight one another, and ourselves, sometimes getting locked in cells when we get too out of hand or become hard to command and control.

Command: dominate (a strategic position) from a superior height.

According to Caroline Myss and others, each of us have within us four primary survival archetypes who are either in their scared or sacred sides and which we will be well served to meet now while feeling safe and relaxed compared to when the stress of life is upon us and the victim, child, prostitute and saboteur within act out of fear instead of faith.

Caroline says these are the aspects of ourselves that "cause us to negotiate away the power of our spirits within the physical world." They also influence how we relate to material power, authority and how we make choices because an archetype is a familiar pattern that gets filled in with energy in a universe that fills every space, either by intention or default. This goes back to our choice to be a REACTOR or CREATOR which use the same letters with very different outcomes.

When we're unaware of these inner characters or personalities they rule the roost and often let fear influence their decision-making processes but with some training we can influence them to work in our favour; the sacred design is there, we just need to retrain ourselves to choose faith instead of FEAR.

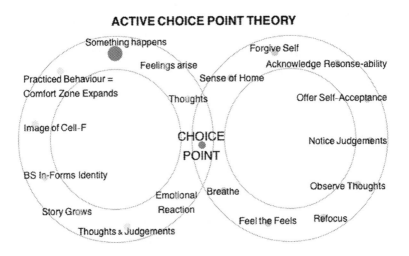

ACTIVE CHOICE POINT THEORY

Something happens
Feelings arise
Practiced Behaviour = Comfort Zone Expands
Sense of Home
Thoughts
Image of Cell-F
CHOICE POINT
BS In-Forms Identity
Emotional Reaction
Breathe
Story Grows
Thoughts & Judgements
Feel the Feels

Forgive Self
Acknowledge Resonse-ability
Offer Self-Acceptance
Notice Judgements
Observe Thoughts
Refocus

Active Choice Point Theory.

Active Choice Point Theory is a concept derived from a conflict resolution skills training program I taught to youth in conflict with the law as my first post-University job. The original concept had two distinct circles which Active Choice Point Theory brings together.

The circle on the left reflects our familiar reactive pattern while the circle on the right offers a creative alternative we can intentionally flow into in order to create new results in our lives. Here's how it works:

1. Something will happen because life is meant to trigger us into new states of being, awareness and choice which are the ABC's of life.
2. Feelings will arise as we interpret the resulting energies in motion (emotions).
3. Thoughts will arise about the feelings we create stories about.
4. Now is where we reach the Choice Point to do what we've always done and get more of what we've always got or do something different and create a different result.
5. An Emotional Reaction that reflects our past level of awareness will arise by default and draw us into familiar mental and emotional territory.
6. Thoughts and Judgements will form that reflect and rely on our past.
7. Our story about life and our place within it will grow because we give it energy.
8. This Belief System In-Forms our Identity and where we feel we belong externally.
9. Our Image of Cell-F gets filled with doubt and False Emotion Appearing Real.
10. This Practiced Behaviour then expands our Comfort Zone in an uncomfortable way.
11. Something will soon happen again and we get to go through this experience again.
12. Feelings will arise as we interpret the resulting energies in motion (emotions).
13. Thoughts will arise about the feelings we create stories about.
14. And now we'll reach the choice point again where we can choose to respond instead.
15. Instead of re-acting as you've always done, pause and take a deep breath to get yourself back in the pre-sent moment.
16. Feel the feels that arise without judgement for they are signals designed to serve.
17. Refocus your attention on the moment you're in without rushing to take action.

18. Observe your thoughts for how they serve you as the script writer of your life.

19. Notice your judgements without falling prey to their devious ways of pulling you out of the present where all of your power exists. Stay in your power.

20. Offer yourself self-acceptance and celebrate yourself for interrupting a pattern that wasn't serving you and recognize how doing so is changing that pattern right now.

21. Acknowledge your ability to respond in a new way to create a better way to respond you can access more easily in the future.

22. Forgive yourself for all the not-now moments you have given your power to and call those fragments back with love, recognizing how emotionally triggered they will be after having been banished from view for so long.

23. Commit to reintegrating them into their sacred side one moment at a time as you create a sense of home they can feel at ease within.

24. Repeat the choice point as something else happens again now choosing your response more intentionally; re-member your power to react or respond in the sacred now moment.

When we dare to climb the spiral staircase of awareness, it's vital that we remember the base is in the same place for NOW is the only moment we ever have to choose how we will use the energetic resources available to us.

We must also recognize how our survival archetypes influence our choice point moment which Caroline Myss' book *Sacred Contracts* describes in detail but the giest is as follows:

The Child archetype establishes our "perceptions of life, safety, nurturing, loyalty and family with core issues relating to dependency and responsibility." When the child is scared it will sacrifice higher level needs for respect and self-actualization in order to belong, feel safe and survive. This archetype in its sacred side is said to be the 'Guardian of Innocence' which helps heal, repair and put a stop to the inner-directed abuse of the wounded child by thinking outside of the box and daring to accept adventures that have no guarantee of success. Adults generally only want to take calculated risks where children are more connected to their inner senses and what feels fun which is how we use our creativity to create a new way forward.

Also remember that innocence and inner-sense are innately connected because our intuitive hunches and sense of knowing without proof are the way our intuition guides us according to our highest good. The child within when scared is disconnected from the sacred side of life or our Divinity so beware whether the child or guardian is sitting on the soul throne of your INNER kingdom.

The Victim archetype is tied to our sense of self-worth, empowerment and personal responsibility and is also the 'Guardian of Self-Esteem.' Caroline says this is the part of us that decides whether we're willing to give up our sense of empowerment to avoid taking responsibility for our independence and will often have a rescuer and punisher on stand-by to keep us distracted from the 'choice point' moments that call us back to the pre-sent where all our power to choose exists.

The Prostitute is the archetype few want to admit to having yet is the part of us that knows the price we're willing to sell ourselves (out) for when scared and also the part that knows our limits too. In its sacred side this is the 'Guardian of Faith' which will help us find a way even when the path has not yet been blazed. Caroline says it is "the ally who puts you on alert every time you contemplate shifting your faith from the Divine to the physical" so that you can align with a vision you desire to give birth to rather than take the easy way out of a challenge.

The Saboteur archetype is the disruptive force within that mirrors our fears of taking responsibility for ourselves and our creations. Acts of courage and trusting our intuition are ways we can silence the scared saboteur within which help it become our "Guardian of Choice." Caroline says "the core issue for the Saboteur is fear of inviting change into your life, change that requires responding in a positive way to opportunities to shape and deepen your spirit."

Laura JE Hamilton

Instead of fearing or revering it we must observe its response to our choices and love ourselves through the process of choosing a thought that will serve us better.

This is what Active Choice Point Theory, with awareness of these survival archetypes within, will help you do while journeying through the ultimate journey called life. And if you can practice settling your nervous system during times when you feel safe then you'll have memory cells to draw on during times of stress like I did and offer from lived experience as you'll be able to do for others with your own stories of resourcefulness too.

INNER Kingdoms, Hidden Gifts & Rescue Missions

Self-image is the mental picture we hold of ourselves and it uses all the beliefs we've stored about our skills, talents, experiences, areas of weakness, hopes, dreams and desires to create it. Self-image expert, Dr. Maxwell Maltz said "changing your self-image does not mean changing yourself, but changing your own mental picture of that self" (*Psychocybernetics*) therefore we don't need to become more than we already are, we simply must see ourselves as capable of more than we previously believed possible and intentionally move our survival archetypes into their sacred side.

We can all temporarily outperform our self-image but if we don't intentionally transform the mental image we hold of ourselves, we will always revert back to behaviours aligned to who we've always seen ourselves to be. Like an elastic band we will be stretched to the edge of our stretch/growth zone and come face to face with the panic zone, which will either see us break through the terror barrier of change or retreat back to the false comforts of home.

Learning to create an inner rabbit hole, as Maltz describes in *Psychocybernetics*, is like finding a transportable sense of home within that helps you feel PEACEFULL despite what is happening around you.

OUR I.N.N.E.R. KINGDOM

Imagine you live in a magnificent castle, with an exquisite interior unparalleled by the beauty of its surroundings. In fact, it is such an exquisite kingdom it doesn't seem to fit in the area where it stands.

You are the keeper of this fine castle and you are proud of it all realizing that the scenery of your surroundings will change over time and you will always be exactly where you are meant to be.

As a child you delighted in the beauty of every aspect of this kingdom and ran excitedly through the corridors amazed by the beauty of all that was yours, until one day you heard a knock on the door and it was one of your beloved tribal members. Remember you were only a child when this knock came, but feel how the truth of what's to come hits you, and where...

Seeing a familiar face at the door you excitedly welcomed them in for a grand tour of your fabulous kingdom and as you showed them around, they 'oohed' and 'awwed' at the magnificence of all they saw until they reached certain areas that made them uncomfortable, especially within the higher floors of your kingdom where they started to feel vulnerable and exposed.

In their discomfort they started making judgements about the parts of your personality, the metaphor this kingdom represents, that they had closed off and judged as not enough within their own kingdom and by the time they left you felt insecure and unsure about what was safe to share and what needed to be held back moving forward.

Taking their judgements personally, you closed the doors to these unapproved of parts of yourself so neither they nor anyone else would be offended by those parts of you again, but over time you did this so many times you have less and less to show when new visitors come around.

Because you had so much space to play with and show off in the beginning you weren't concerned with how each 'shut down' experience was shaping your inner realm and yet over time each knock on the door became anxiety-inducing because you came to realize the judgements that came with each of them and you weren't sure how much more of yourself you could sacrifice in order to prove your enoughness.

Instead of wanting to share your brilliance with others you learned to tone yourself down and try to blend in so as to not become a target of attack or criticism but in the process you became disenchanted with the beauty of all you are; their judgements made you feel unsafe within your own kingdom and over time you forgot just how magnificent you truly are.

*A visualization rooted in Debbie Ford's book *The Dark Side of the Light Chasers.*

A GIFT IN DISGUISE

I once connected with a man who suffered from low self- esteem that manifested itself as a stuttering problem. He told me he had always been self-conscious about his looks and to top it off he could never get his words out how he wanted to. I'd helped him purchase a video package to grow his business and after filming the video he came back to share his disappointment in how he'd done and the poor investment it had been for him, given his lack of confidence or faith in himself. Fortunately, there was a lull in the crowd so I had time to walk him through his inner kingdom and see his 'problem' from a different perspective which can serve us all to consider.

As I actively listened to his stories of not-enoughness, I saw the little boy inside of him that was stammering for his attention and re-framed how much this part of himself loved him. I helped him understand that for all these years, his stutter had been this little boy's attempt to keep him safe because if he didn't believe he could properly express himself, he would never have to fully grow into all that he could be; playing small and keeping his head beneath the parapet, to this small and immature part of him, felt safer than standing up and taking charge of his life. His child archetype was living in its scared side and was unable to shift into its sacred role as the guardian of innocence without his support and acceptance.

Together we connected with this stuttering child within who was desperate to be loved and who loved him so deeply he was willing to be hated in order to keep them all safe from a child's limited vantage point.

I encouraged him to change his feelings toward this part of himself so that instead of resenting and rejecting it, he could see how his stutter had been his inner child's way of protecting him for all those years. Instead of resenting himself for a problem that reinforced his story of not-enoughness, it was time for him to retrieve this version of himself from the room he had locked it away in all those years ago.

Guiding him through the corridors of a mostly dark and closed down castle, we arrived at the room where a five year old version of him had sat for more than half a century. As he unlocked the door and reluctantly entered a room he had judged and tried to deny for most of his life, he returned to the place where he had started and saw it with new eyes because he finally had compassion for this part of himself; by getting down on the floor to connect with this hurting aspect of himself he was able to offer himself acceptance as he was and stop resenting himself for the behaviour this part of him had learned to use to call for attention (and love) in a dysfunctional way. He was finally able to see his 'problem' from a new perspective and stop resenting the symptom of an underlying cause he'd previously denied which kept it charged up.

The story of not-enough that had ruled his inner kingdom for all those years was just the habitual thought pattern he had bought into before he could consciously participate in the creative process and now they had a chance to change their story together. By finding compassion for this little boy he understood that he could be more gentle with himself in those moments when his stutter showed up to let him know his inner child was scared and seeking love. By discovering this while feeling seen and safe with me, he gained a tool he could use during future reactive moments to bring more peace to his perspective and give himself what he was unconsciously craving.

It was a turning point. His stutter had become a gift in an instant, all because he was willing to shift his perspective of it. I encouraged him to invite this little boy out of the room, and after some coaxing they emerged, hand in hand, loving the part of himself that loved him more than anything.

The abandoned and rejected parts of us misbehave because they are trapped in the rooms we shut down when we were told they weren't good enough to exist in such a beautiful space. This is what this little boy had become for this beautiful man who was brave enough to seize the moment despite the setting; we must dare to do the same for the magick of the moment is spontaneous, just like the child within is meant to be, and the more we allow ourselves to stay present and play with life as it arises, the safer we will feel to be ourselves.

Each metaphoric room in the kingdom of our personality that was criticized became a threat to our ability to belong to the tribe and changing to accommodate them was a survival mechanism we used to feel at home where we were. What we failed to understand, because it's not part of our socialization process, is that home is not a place but a space within our heart. Home is where the heart is rather than where we hang our hat at night or pay for the privilege of pretending to own in a world where mortgages are debt pledges to corp(s)es with no accountability for deceiving those who made the mistake of thinking a house was a home.

Mort: the note sounded on a horn when the quarry (a rich source) is killed.

Gage: a valued object deposited as a guarantee of good faith.

So let us dare to see how the journey inward to the hearth of our heart is the greatest legacy we can truly leave because of how it helps us come into wholeness and bless the world with authentic presence and warmth that calls others back to the pre-sent moment with love.

Hearth: a vital or creative center; the floor of a fire-place.

Bruce Lipton's book *The Honeymoon Effect* uses a scientific explanation for the shift away from being like a 'chemical compound' looking to bond with others through dysfunction to being a 'noble gas' that is already whole and complete without need for another but who can still enjoy vibing at higher levels with good company. There is a big difference between needing someone or something to make us feel complete compared to desiring company with others on their own journey to higher levels of awareness that make space for one another in the process; in-secure people need things, while people with INNER security desire to give birth to life in a new way with others who want to play at a higher level too. It's the difference between being a re-actor versus a creator which use the same letters with a completely different impact.

The more functional and balanced we become the more 'homey' we will feel to others who don't feel secure on their own which is currently the majority because few know how to do the inner excavating required to return to their heart centre without fear of what they'll find.

Be conscious of 'homies' who want to take more than they're willing to give back in return for your investment into them and beware of when you become a taker too. I went through a phase of taking energy from those who were willing to invest into me and then I spent it freely on others without refueling the source of my upliftment; I drained many of these relationships and broke trust with the ones I took from that I can only hope to rebuild bridges where gaps currently exist. We do the best we can with what we know at the time, or we don't, and the higher in consciousness we are the faster our karma comes back to us.

Feeling insecure makes our experience of home feel unsafe while INNER security helps us feel safe to be ourselves and give others permission to do the same.

We may not always get it right but the more INNER kingdom rescue missions we are willing to go on the safer our INNER world will become and the freer we will feel to support others through their organic unfoldment without getting triggered or taking things personally. This is how we become allies without need for wars to unite us and truly keep our home lands safe and secure as we all wish to feel sure of.

The Sacred Sojourn of the Soul

20

The Sacred Sojourn of the Soul is a twelve-step process, as so many in today's world are, only this one is designed to call you present by re-membering that life is sacred and all-ways happening NOW, until we're no longer alive to live in the pre-sent moment.

> *Sacred: highly valued and important; entitled to reverence and respect*
> *Sojourn: a temporary stay (for none of us make it out of life alive)*

It's about recognizing that life is a solo journey that we enter and leave alone but get to play alongside others who are also on their soul's respective journey of evolution where we are meant to aide and assist one another in learning the lessons our souls need in order to uplevel the WEBs we are weaving our lives with.

It's also about breaking things down to the ridiculous so we no longer overlook hidden meanings and patterns within things, particularly the words we are spell casting our lives with. Remember that on our gravestones the day our journey started and ended is likely to be mentioned but the whole of our lives will be covered by the dash in between. So while the big events and adventures may seem to be the landmarks we track, our greatest growth will take place in the leadup to them, moments during them, and the aftermath of them when we connect the dots as to why things unfold as they do in preparation for what's to come next.

The letters J-O-Y start and end the word journey but an URNE is what is left in between for us to decide which wolf we will feed our energy to as the Cherokee parable goes. While 'urn' has come to be associated with the vessel a cremated body is laid to rest in after the soul has left this 3D REALITY we call life, we must see that the added E for energy turns that vessel into a 'ballot box' for us to vote with in this one life we get to lead as us.

The Sacred Sojourn of the Soul.

Phase 1: Preparation

This phase prepares us to move from pre-contemplation into action that leads to growth.

1. **HOME** - This is our current comfort zone reflecting who we believe ourselves to be, how we fit in the world and who we fit in with. While we may not be comfortable where we are it's familiar and provides us with a false sense of comfort, often bound by obligation and duty. It's where higher-level needs

for growth and contribution are sacrificed for lower level ones like survival, safety and belonging with people we let vote on what is possible for us.

This costs self-respect we don't usually like to own up to losing and so we do our best to push down our heart-felt desires so we can more comfortably lie in the bed we made for ourselves, without feeling boxed in by limitations we often deny living with.

Learning to feel at home within ourselves is how we develop a portable sense of INNER security we can bring with us into the stretch zone life is always calling us to enter without losing our sense of connection to those we love in the process, which must include our cells. Achieving self-love often requires going on an adventure or few that stretches our familiar reality so we can learn to trust ourselves to feel safe in unfamiliar environments, states and stages of life even when they aren't comfortable. This is how we expand our comfort zone.

2. **THE CALL** - It can come from within or be triggered by a connection that gets the heart racing, but it calls for change that requires leaving your familiar comfort zone in order to reach your next level of awareness as a soulfull being having a hue-man experience. Remember that with every new level of experience and awareness you will encounter new devils, higher rent and new neighbours but you wouldn't be called to make the change if you didn't have the ability to fulfill it but your commitment will be tested to see how committed you are to living that which you feel called to be, do or have in this life. Trust yourself and the Guardians within for spiritual guides and allies are cheering for you on the 'other side' of the veils, moving on your behalf whether you can see it or not. Trust is a huge part of heeding the call for expansion; trust you wouldn't be called to it if you didn't have the ability to fulfill it. Just be sure to feel into what part

of you is speaking as personal experience calls me to say: our plan and the creator's plan often have very different timelines and we are not in control of how it will all unfold. We can influence it by consistent action, just aim to be in charge of the inspired actions you choose to take daily instead of trying to control the details; being in control is an illusion that keeps us contracted under bridges meant to be walked over whereas being in charge is about commanding your energy which are very different experiences to live through and recall later.

3. **VEILING THE UNREST** - This is how we get in our own way and let the stories we tell ourselves about ourselves, or believe others are telling about us, get to and under-mine us. It shows up as the voice of self-doubt and insecurity that weakens the ground we stand on and often drives us toward coping mechanisms of choice whether that be a substance, behaviour, reaction or device. Anything that takes you out of the moment you are in is reinforcing the pattern of self-sabotage. Until we slice through or lift these veils they will keep us playing small so beware of the patterns you notice from the past that show up in the moment you try something new. Your survival archetypes are terrified of change until you prove yourself capable of the task at hand which only comes through experience. You're going to have to do it afraid and beware of the scared side of yourself as you embrace the unfamiliar.

4. **MEETING THE ONE** - In times of doubt and uncertainty, when we aren't sure we have what it takes to accomplish the task we're being called to, meeting someone who believes in us can be what it takes for us to commit to the journey and step out into the unknown. They will hold up a mirror of possibility, by their example as one who dared to follow the call they heard, and can give you the courage to do your best to believe in the beauty of your dreams too. Each time

you go after your dreams and persist in achieving them you will strengthen this part of yourself and get to meet the guru within, but until then you can join PEACEFULL INNER Warriors United and Untied from the illusions that keep us playing small who are daring to see the "I'm possible" in what may feel impossible or impassable in the moment your humanly-self approaches it. Dare to push through and you will co-create a reality you love living, just know that you'll come up against the shadow within that seems way scarier when you give it your power.

Phase 2: The Valley of Transformation

This second phase will take us on an adventure that will change our beliefs about ourselves and how we fit in the world because we will gain experiences that only exist beyond the limits of our previous comfort zone, and once stretched it rarely returns to the same form it had before. During this phase others can encourage us from the sidelines but no one can go through the full transformation with us for it must be walked by the one living the experience alone.

5. **ACCEPTING THE CALL** - Stepping into the liminal phase of change that takes us out of our comfort zone and places us firmly in the heart of growth can be a breath-taking experience. It's like the first few moments of skydiving when the air is rushing so fast you can't hardly catch your breath and you have no choice but to keep going because you're all in. It is the point in our journey where we leave behind the world we've always known, and who we knew ourselves to be within it, in order to try something we have no guarantee will work out the way we hope it will but we know we'll have stories to share when we're through. Do it afraid and know that you were brave to even get here in the first place so dare to push through the discomfort!

6. **TRIALS AND TRIBULATIONS** - The valley of transformation is full of situations, circumstances and relationships that will stretch and grow us in preparation for the battle that is ahead. They teach us the rules of the new world we are in and offer in-sights into the new world we are in the process of co-creating for ourselves. The teachers we meet here come with varying lessons and teaching styles which are all inherently designed to help us prepare for the unseen forces we will face ahead, so even when it hurts be grateful for the opportunity to strengthen spiritual muscles you didn't even know you had or would need. Also, dare to separate the teacher from the teaching so you can get the lesson without needing a more advanced teacher to school you in the pattern and recognize that life's teachers cover different ground depending on how high you're willing to climb the spiral staircase of awareness; the higher you go, the more advanced your curriculum will be. A feather teacher will show up first, then a wool sweater teacher that is more irritating, then a sandpaper teacher who will scrub the surface layers off, before the two-by-four teacher that hits you aside the head in hopes of saving you from the bus or train that's more difficult to recover from. Get the lesson from the pattern and leave the dirt behind for the treasure was all you went in to find; separate your energy from the memory by letting the energies in motion from the experience flow in the present so you can reclaim your power.

7. **THE DARK KNIGHT OF THE EGO** – This is when the Edging God Out part of us takes a knee to something or someone less than the creator of all by letting Earthly matters take us out of the pre-sent NOW moment. Knights must bow to someone acting as something more than they are by themselves in order to be granted a status the man then believes himself to be; he must then toe the line to maintain his status which can be taken from him by a force outside of

his control or influence at any time. It is a very dangerous place to find oneself indeed which is why greed for outer attainment drives the man away from his divine nature. This is where we must fight our attachments with external identifiers like status, prestige, people, wealth and things.

8. **THE DARK-LIGHT OF THE SOUL** – This is where we will face our shadow aspects that don't want to be exposed lest they be deposed from the INNER throne room of the kingdom within. The survival archetypes that have tended toward living in their scared side will be called out to face the light of their true nature which only feels scary because it's unfamiliar and the ego already feels like it has lost too much. We must now choose to call fragments of ourselves back present and offer acceptance to the 'emotional personas' that are emerging from rooms within our INNER kingdom that can only remember feeling unloved, unlovable, unworthy and unreceived. These repressed and denied aspects do not know how to express their passion, enthusiasm, authenticity, clarity and encouragement in functional or healthy ways and carry much shame, regret, guilt and resentment for all the crosses they have been carrying for as long as they can remember.

There is no sense of safety or security during this INNER battle so it is the leading cause of what some would consider a spiritual depression that often sends us back to veiling the unrest or seeking professional assistance to get back in a box our consciousness no longer fits in. Unfortunately, we can't un-see what we've seen or unknow what we've woken up to and trying to forget what we set out to achieve when we left the comfort zone before only fragments our power so we have less presence to call on in future now moments.

We can't escape this enemy because it lives within us and knows all of our secrets; this is where the scared saboteur has a chance to become the Guardian of Choice but we have to choose which wolf to feed in the moment our scared and sacred sides are fighting for the throne.

No one feels equipped to go through this because it is the equivalent of journeying into the innermost cave where a dragon protects the jewels and riches; to get the gold we must slay the dragon and that's terrifying but no more so than failing to bring forth the gift we came here to bless the world with. So even though we will tremble in our boots, we must face this head on like a buffalo does a storm as it is the only animal that runs into the eye of a storm and finds clear skies and a rainbow on the other side while the rest tire from trying to outrun it, much like so many do their destiny.

Saint Francis of Assisi is said to have been seen physically battling his demons and the supernatural forces that tried to block him from discovering the golden nature within him and I will always remember my own experience of the equivalent as a mystic without a monastery. Loved ones may stand nearby to offer support and prayers, which will help, but they can't feel the fear for us or help us access the inner reserves of faith, strength or self-belief that are required to face the darkness within us; we must survive ourselves and the battle will be like none we've experienced before but remember this: you would not be led to it if you couldn't make it through it. Where there is a will there is a way so dare to feel the FEAR fully so you can say "get thee behind me Satan" as the great sages did by moving through the discomfort of their shadow side to reach salvation in the sacred.

9. **THE PHOENIX PROCESS** - This is where surrender is required. This phase is when we burn up our attachments to the agreements we made with False Emotion Appearing Real to play small for the sake of fitting into a box that would bury us alive if we let it. This is what our words will do if we do not become the authority of our own identity regardless of the statuses applied to us by others who have forgot who and whose they are too.

We must walk into the fire of forgiveness that will transmute our pain into gains others will benefit from when the process is complete but we cannot do this for the sake of others yet. Now is not the time to compete or compare our process to anyone else's for no one goes through it the same way for we all came to plan-et Earth missing parts we came to reclaim.

Confused people will always try to contaminate the clarity of others because they are covered in mud like the Golden Buddha statue whose natural state of beauty, worth and genuine value were discovered by accident.

There is a story of a village in Tibet who worshipped a Buddha statue that appeared to be made of clay. Eventually, the statue was scheduled to be moved and after an unintended accident, its gift was revealed to the world. Centuries before, the Burmese had invaded Tibet and were looting all valuables from monasteries and temples throughout the country. Before they reached this particular sacred site, the Tibetan monks there had diligently worked to cover a golden statue with undesirable materials, making it appear worthless and not worth the effort of moving. When the soldiers arrived, they took what valuables they could see and killed everyone, including all who knew about the Buddha's golden nature.

In a shell the Buddha sat for all those years, overlooked and unloved for what it truly was. When moving day came, the Buddha's unsuspecting weight snapped the ropes and pulleys, dropping the statue and knocking some of the mud and stucco away.

Afraid to get in trouble the workers inspected the damage to see if it was repairable but instead saw golden light streaming out from the cracks where the sun struck. One brave and curious man chiselled some of the surface away to discover the true prize hidden within and so it was that the statue was once again seen for what it always was underneath the illusions.

This is the sacred process of turning our scared aspects into sources of inner strength and inspiration we can reference in future situations and also share with others once we've completed the transformation process.

We will not be the same as we were before this and as we approach the pyre of our own transformation, we know it. Go anyway and be transformed whether others see the value in doing so or not; you've already been through so much, what is the use of turning back now?

Phase 3: Ownership

This is the final phase of change that will see us become the one we were waiting for and were called to re-member ourselves to be the whole time.

10. **THE BIG I (INTEGRATION OF A NEW STORY)** - After emerging from the valley of Transformation, we must assimilate the lessons we learned from the death of our former self-image and write new stories about ourselves and the world around us. Our ego will do its best to undermine us for a final time by holding us hostage to all that didn't go as planned, yet we have already faced death and survived, creating memory cells that will be there for us forever after. Now we must take our experiences to the quarry station of our INNER mine and find the rewards that were hidden within all that we went through to help us re-member who and whose we've always been.

Our experiences help us re-member that true power comes from within so now we must practice presence and re-establish a relationship with our pre-sense (intuition).

11. **EMBODIMENT OF A NEW E-SIGNATURE** - Changing our energetic signature means raising our normal point of view and frequency to a higher level, along with the standards

we'll settle for in our relationships with others and also ourselves. The status quo may still resonate for others around us but now we see the price we pay for playing a role someone else assigned to us and our WEB is strong enough to break the mold that used to hold us back.

It's a new way of living in the present where before we thought we needed to earn our way now we see we own the riches dis-covered within and no one can take them away. Our sense of self-worth, self-esteem and self-belief has been intentionally re-structured because we took responsibility for our cells and the essence we now embody which can be felt by those we come into contact with. Others will feel the shift we've made because we no longer need their approval or acceptance to stand fully in our power. After all we've been through we have gained respect for ourselves and no longer settle for poor treatment by those who wish to diminish us to make themselves feel better about where they choose to stay. We no longer try to rescue people by getting in the ditch with them; instead we can walk to the edge and offer them a hand we're unattached as to whether they accept or not. This is the art of non-attachment.

We have become individuals who honour the path others choose and refuse to sacrifice our own honour in order to meet them at lower frequency states because now our normal state is at a higher level and shrinking to conform is more uncomfortable than before. Our circle gets smaller as we raise our standards because few are willing to pay the price to get where we've been and now choose to be seen without FEAR of who may be offended by our empowered state, yet those who do are quality people who will be able to support us when we go through the sacred sojourn again because we always do.

12. **CONTRIBUTION** - This is when we discover we are back where we started as the victor of the battle waged within ourselves and the world as a result. Many do not make it this

far because scarcity mentality will encourage us to keep our lessons to ourselves so as to not give others an edge or added advantage they may use to rise above us but those who dare to share a story that inspires others by example (lived experience rather than just theory) can be assured it will help someone in their moment of need.

It's like the story of a man who was jogging along a beach where thousands of starfish had washed onto the shore and in the distance he could see the silhouette of a man tossing one starfish after another back into the water. When he finally neared the man he slowed down to inform him the whole beachline was full of them and his efforts weren't going to make a difference in the scheme of things. The man carried on and as he picked up yet another starfish, he reminded the jogger that may be true but it'll make a world of difference to this one.

And so will be true of the tale you live to tell another who needs to hear your story to make it through their own. Hard-won wisdom is far more power-full than knowledge from theories that sound good but haven't been applied as these theories were to me when I started writing the book that rewrote me before the world got to read the book that took five years to write in a month; life is not a dress rehearsal yet sometimes we need a lot of practice to separate the wheat (value) from the shaft (experience) so our morals have greater meaning.

All of it is purposeful if we're willing to breakthrough instead of break down as many times as it takes to become the one who did.

We all go through this process many times throughout our lives and each time we do we accrue more of the gold life holds for us. Finding ways to be authentically present with others as they go through this process too is the fastest way for us to feel valuable as the social creatures we are. Growth and contribution are the highest expressions of self-actualization within the hierarchy of motivational needs so if ever you get discouraged or lose heart along the way remember the gift of inspiration your lived story will be to others and also your future self.

Every time we get back on the horse after we've fallen off, daring to try again where FEAR would say stay home instead, we add to our WEB of self-worth, self-esteem and self-belief which is priceless, as are you. Keep pushing through the terror barrier of your former self-image and watch the invisible glass ceiling that previously limited you rise to meet you instead. For that is the WEB we'll eventually benefit from after putting in the work of building it.

Toxic Loads, Colours Of Right & The Highrise Of Emotional Awareness

21

Our soul's journey only ends when the spark leaves our eyes because we have fragmented ourselves too much to stay pre-sent in the vessel our soul came to planet Earth in. The more environmental toxins and pollutants we take into our bodies, the less functional we are and the poorer our health and magnetic potential will be. Health is wealth because without it we can't enjoy what riches we accrue nor can we stay focused on our desires if pain is in the way so becoming more response-able stewards of our energetic resources matters in this life!

While living in England I worked as an Independent Organic Skincare Consultant with the home division of Neal's Yard Remedies for a time and absolutely loved it. I took as many trainings as I could attend and even managed to win an incentive trip to Rhode Island and Dallas my first year with the company which is a story in itself for another time.

During that chapter of my life I created an informative report to impart what I was learning to prospective customers about the chemical ingredients hidden in commonly used products. I felt people needed to be aware of the fact we all carry a 'toxic load' within our bodies, just as nature does, and now it's essential we connect the dots between the physical, emotional, mental and spiritual influences we are currently dealing with.

But what is a toxic load?

Also known as 'body burden,' a toxic load includes all the toxins our body has accumulated through environmental pollutants and ingested sources throughout our lives, remnants of which get stored in the organs if we don't support our cells in eliminating the waste. A high toxic load takes a toll on our nervous and immune systems because our body cannot process these foreign intruders and over time the build-up can lead to dis-ease (cellular disharmony caused by toxic influences).

When our body receives a toxin that it does not recognize, it can't 'file' it appropriately so will either send it to the organ meant to deal with similar matters (materials) or it will continue to circulate through our system as free radicals that cause damage to all it inter-acts with inside of us.

Louise L Hay wrote a great book on this called *You Can Heal Your Life* which associates physical ailments with emotional issues, offering affirmations to change the story creating the cellular disharmony within the body. Charging these statements with energy (emotion) is how to move them from the conscious mind of reason-ability into the subconscious mind of feelings which are the way we interpret the energies in motion within and around us. I was first recommended that book by my Reiki Master when I was 16 dealing with a secret eating disorder I'd developed when 'the most popular boy in school' asked me out and I outperformed my low self-image so unconsciously got caught in a WEB of toxic BS. In order to "have my cake and eat it too" I started binging on junk food some days after school and purging it so I didn't wear it but I gained weight anyway, the guy dumped me right before New Year's Eve and I'd picked up a new reason to hate myself even more. I carried on with it for several years until part way through University I refused to let myself escape the consequences of my choices where food was concerned any longer and that was that. I eventually stopped obsessing about my weight or the foods I ate and returned to my pre-bulimic weight which I've largely maintained ever since by focusing my attention on my health and how I feel instead of what the scale says; when I'm in tune with my body I don't burden myself and extra weight tends to correspond with longer wait times dealing with the emotional cause of physical effects. A high-vibrational diet is the fastest way to drop weight physically and mentally because emotional baggage doesn't resonate at higher levels of a theory I call the Highrise of Emotional Awareness.

I've come to see the mind as a trap we've been conditioned to focus on so that we fall prey to the emotions we've denied or tried to suppress in the name of 'toxic positivity' that only masks hidden False Emotion Appearing Real (FEAR) that take us into not-now moments where our power to create something better is limited. We must see how energies in motion need to move while 'states of being' need nothing to change to be fully present where we are.

The Highrise of Emotional Awareness is a framework to functionally maneuver emotional states and states of being present with greater awareness and relatability using the "Emotional Guidance System" by Esther 'Abraham' Hicks applied to the concept that an apartment building has the same address top to bottom but is a completely different experience depending on which floor of the building we're at in the moment or where we normally stay within our consciousness.

Emotions usually show up with momentums of energy from the past or a future we FEAR and draw near to beware of. If we are willing to disconnect from the stories that take us out of the present where our power to choose exists then we can reclaim authority over our lives and write a script that will serve us better than the ones a less conscious aspect of ourselves created before we'd lived and learned to discern information for how it serves us.

Active Choice Point Theory is a useful tool to reference in relation to the emotions and states of being because no matter how many times we've let the trauma, drama and fear win in the past, each time we check ourselves before we wreck ourselves, our relationships or our ability to be present in the now we build cells of recognition (familiarity) that help us create new patterns that will serve us better moving forward.

Archetypes are fuelled by energy we've stored up as memories that still hold a charge which is why we can be triggered into the 'not-now' so easily if we allow our programs (patterns) to run us instead of consciously running them. Changing patterns requires effort upfront because our energy is used to following the familiar storylines we've told for so long and got charged up by re-living time and again simply because we unconsciously invested our sense of identity into them and we've built so many bonds with others using them that the ego fears changing. It's invested in its habits just like the nuns whose identity comes from wearing their habit which is the uni-form the woman wears when working for the church in that position. It's a symbol of respect we've been taught to revere but would be well served to consider how the habits we choose define our sense of identity similarly, even if we don't officially wear the garb.

Getting acquainted with the emotions already active within you is a necessary starting point in the reclamation of your power because empower-ment is a matter of "giving (someone) the authority or power to do something" by helping them take charge of their mind by choosing mental constructs that will serve instead of disempower.

Recognizing how the emotions charge up mental patterns will help to make friends out of the energies within so they can help call back our power in the moment we are in based on how we feel (resonate) with people and situations that show up for us. Instead of letting ourselves get carried away by the stories of the past or a future we feel full of fear about, what if instead we focused on what we can do to up-level our own vibration to a higher level in the moment we are in so that together we contribute to the shift in collective consciousness that lifts the normal state of all to a more peace-full level?

JMT Founding President Paul Martinelli used to say "a rising tide lifts all boats" and our consciousness is the same. Our frequency determines how frequently we are able to tune into truth by balancing awareness and will-power within the magnetic centre of our heart which manifests our de-sires like a radio tuning into different channels or stations.

We are each the equivalent of a radio station sending out signals to the Universe that are received by the Grand Overall Designer and then returned to us using cooperative parts which are the people, places and things in our respective environments.

Think of each emotion like a channel we dial into that plays all the stories related to that energy in motion from the past or from stories we've heard others tell that trigger cells of recognition and call us to tune into that frequency more intently. That's what resonance is; relate-ability based on familiarity that allows us to bond and connect through the energy in motion we are dialled into with others who are also 'tuned in' to that metaphoric station.

Also recognize that lower frequencies pull higher frequencies down easier than higher frequencies can lift lower frequencies up if they don't wish to raise the bar they've got familiar with frequenting. Whether that be the pub/bar frequented to enter altered states by influence of outside sources, or the BAR that legal professionals swear an oath of allegiance to protect and act on be-half of which compromises their integrity as men and women who must re-present a coloured reality to profit the house of the overreaching corps(e), or whether that be the bar we limbo under or leap over as part of a game we take on shame for when we miss the mark; these are all examples of glass ceilings our full commitment to being present can help us break through together as we must now do.

Secret societies have recognized the power of emotions and they've been weaponized against us to keep the bar low but the game of life is not just child's play and emotions are not meant to be controlled in the dysfunctional way we've been trained.

Sympathy and empathy are distinctly different ways to relate to one another that we must now make clear so we can practice connecting at higher and more functional levels than the lower levels we've got comfortable connecting on using dysfunction to seal our bonds and fates by default.

The best analogy for the difference between sympathy and empathy that I've heard is that sympathy is like seeing someone in a ditch and then crawling into the ditch to be with them when the reality is we have to get ourselves out of the ditch to help them out lest we lift them out and get left behind because they lack the strength to help us out after we helped them. Empathy is seeing someone in the ditch and walking to the edge to offer them a hand up without lowering our vibration to meet them where they are even if they desperately want us to get down and dirty in a story they could change their relationship to if they were willing to raise their state of being present to see it from a different vantage point.

Professionals are trained to limit their connectivity with clients to not get attached which often lacks heart because the textbook way can only train so far. Taking on the emotional state of an-other doesn't help the one playing victim who is caught in a disempowered trap of codependence on outer circumstances but holding a space where they can feel witnessed without supporting the pattern of externalizing their power is a fine balance we can only feel our way through because each of us are unique and require different kinds of support.

The tipping point between uplifting and depressing emotional spirals is between presence and connection to the not-now when our over-active minds covertly seek complexity for entertainment purposes which is why boredom is the devil's playground.

Pay close attention to your level of presence for that is how you can catch yourself before you wreck yourself most easily. If you are in your head you are not in your heart which is where your healing starts. Your breath is the tool you can all-ways use to call yourself back to the present moment where your entire life is lived, unless you let the devil in the details take you into a not-present moment where your power is placed outside of yourself and you're back in the lower frequencies where drama, trauma, and victimhood prevail.

Highrise of Emotional Awareness

1. Love, PEACE, JOY, Knowledge, Empowerment, Freedom
2. Passion
3. Enthusiasm, Eagerness, Happiness
4. Positive Expectation, Belief
5. Optimism
6. Hopefulness
7. Contentment (Bottom of States of Being - Upward Spiral)
8. Boredom (Top of States of E-Motion - Downward Spiral)
9. Pessimism
10. Frustration, Irritation, Impatience
11. Overwhelment
12. Disappointment
13. Doubt
14. Worry
15. Blame
16. Discouragement
17. Anger
18. Revenge
19. Hatred, Rage
20. Jealousy
21. Insecurity, Guilt, Unworthiness
22. FEAR, Grief, Depression, Despair, Powerlessness

By: Laura JE Hamilton

The Highrise of Emotional Awareness.

In the basement we feel buried by *False Emotion Appearing Real, grief, depression and powerlessness (22)* which limits our ability to create something better than the reality we can see. This is where the Victim lives in its scared side hoping a rescuer will come to save us from the punisher who is pressing down on us. Here we feel boxed in by all the limitations and liabilities we feel confined by in this emotionally contracted state; our emotions are weaponized against us here because we don't know how to cope with the momentums of energies in motion that take us out of our power and drag us into all the not-now moments we have yet to forgive ourselves for. We can only go up from here.

On the ground floor of *insecurity, guilt and unworthiness (21)* we live in a glass house where everything feels like a threat to our safety and survival. Our inner sense of security is compromised by guilt we have over circumstances outside of our control and yet we keep beating ourselves up, catching ourselves in a WEB of limiting BS that may have kept us safe in the past but is only causing lasting damage to the kingdom within. Whatever happened before does not need to confine you any longer than it already has. You were born worthy despite what this corrupted world has said; collect the garbage BS strewn all around this open concept room and create a new choice point experience.

Jealousy (20) comes next because the first floor up from insecurity, guilt and unworthiness is still close enough to the streets to feel vulnerable. We see people walking around in the streets below us and wonder what their home life is like, trying to peer into surrounding buildings to see what others have that we might want or need; John Maxwell says you might want to do what I'm doing but you won't want to do what I've done to get here. When in a jealous state of mind we just see the surface and forget to ask what went into getting that which is now present; we can't see the forest through the trees at this level and are limited by living on the effect end of the cause and effect equation.

Hatred and rage (19) come next because we are blinded by this rigid state of mind that keeps us tied to something in the past which we can't seem to get over. Our hatred keeps us from separating the lesson from the experience so the whole memory is off limits and rage is our guard dog. There is no reasoning with this energy in motion because so much of it has been denied it's always waiting for a chance to be let out; causing harm to those who unintentionally step on this land mine within our emotional terrain make us hate ourselves even more; here we project what we're infected with.

Revenge (18) is how we try to steal power from those around us and within us as a result of resentment and resistance. Our limited vision of the present clouds our view of the future and we forget how mean karma can be when it gives us a taste of our own toxic medicine.

Revenge is the act of hurting someone in return for hurting us but we often fail to see how we are actually punishing ourselves by scorching the Earth around us by acting against our better judgement. This emotional state adds fuel to the floors beneath and costs a lot of energy to dwell in for any length of time.

Anger (17) is an energy in motion that can move us to express the negative emotions we are carrying within and can help us change negative patterns if we are willing to channel it into a sacred direction. It is considered a secondary emotion because it's generally caused by frustration, irritation, abuse or unfairness. It's the energy in motion that gets us moving, it's just necessary for us to choose whether we are willing to feel our way through it to call our lost power back to the present or whether we will let the momentums of energies from the past drag us down and out of the now.

Discouragement (16) is when we lose heart and presence of mind to find hope for something better than we're presently able to tune into. It's a loss of confidence or enthusiasm, downheartedness or dispiritedness because too much energy is placed in a not-now moment. Getting re-centred and grounded helps because it helps us shift gears and see the fears masquerading as truth taking up residence within our minds.

Blame (15) is when we place our power outside of ourselves by giving someone or something credit for something we see as happening to us instead of for us. Victims ride around on the blame and complain train which only lead to lower level emotions so dare to reframe your circumstances to consider how the challenges you are facing may actually be helping you turn a corner and reach for higher levels of awareness within this highrise of energies in motion.

Worry (14) is like a rocking chair that takes a lot of effort but gets you nowhere; here we forget that nowhere and 'now here' are only a space apart but can make a world of difference to your INNER state and heart presence. Dare to step into doubt instead and get clear what you're uncertain you can achieve.

Doubt (13) is uncertainty, distrust or lack of confidence in a situation you aren't sure about but how could you be when you haven't had it or experienced it before? Doubt is a natural part of the growth process because you don't know whether you've got what it takes to make your dreams come true, but you must remember that dreams are made a few sizes too big so you can grow into them. Consider it like a baby who will grow into a man one day; the baby doesn't know how it's going to do it or how long it will take to reach his full-grown status but if allowed to unfold naturally he will get there and the same is true for you.

Dare to feel your *disappointment (12)* for not being there yet but keep moving in the direction of your dreams anyway remembering a dream will seem out of reach until you have it and then you will soon find yourself dreaming new dreams instead of basking in the experience of reaching that which was previously out of reach. Don't fall in the trap of doubting you're on the right track lest you slip further down the slippery slope of all the floors you've already climbed. Also remember that each state of e-motion is temporary so use your choice point to flip the dis-appointment to the side.

Overwhelment (11) is the feeling of too many new sensations hitting your nervous system at once without knowing how to filter them. Outer circumstances or the momentums of energies in motion from the past that all show up in the present to be dealt with can feel like 'too much' all at once. It's a sign of growth and being challenged to grow beyond your previous comfort zone so trust the process and know that you wouldn't be called to it if you didn't have the capacity to fulfill it. Break bigger tasks and goals into smaller, bite sized chunks, and do as much as you can in the moment while still giving yourself breaks when needed to recharge and come back with energy to face all that's coming up to be transmuted and replaced.

Frustration, Irritation and Impatience (10) are common side effects of the fast-paced, instant gratification cult-u-re lived in by most. We want big results quickly and expect fast resolutions without dealing with the discomfort of changing our circumstances. Adjustments are required internally and externally for with every new level comes new devils, higher rent and new neighbours; those are hardly comfortable circumstances to face and we're doing it every single day without giving ourselves credit for how well we are adjusting our cells and our self-image as we move through life. I've lived here for years as my 'normal state of emotional experience' and suggest recognizing how far we've already come to have reached this level; gratitude journals can help call our focus back to the present so dare to grab your pen and start where you are, giving thanks for all that is great and all that has offered you contrast too. Clarity often comes as a result of getting sick and tired of being sick and tired so find the lesson your frustration, irritation and impatience are offering you and make space for its replacement.

Pessimism (9) is the tendency to look for or expect the worst and is our in-built safeguard against growth. This is where the scared saboteur teams up with the prostitute to negotiate how much more energy we're willing to call back to the present moment without denying any of the feelings showing up from within us. The future seems bleak because we don't know what to expect moving forward and yet we can't go back to the way things were before we knew what we were growing into so try not to let feeling jaded get you down. You are in the final stretch and your break through is right around the corner; stay committed and see your pessimism as a sign your ego is scared to give up the life it knew before you got where you've been working to get for so long. You are three feet from gold, using the infamous tale of the Darby brothers from *Think and Grow Rich* who gave up a fully loaded gold mine because they didn't know about fault lines; calling on support at this stage may help you see things from a vantage point you hadn't considered before and help you find the gold you're within reach of.

Boredom (8) is a danger zone because we want to be entertained or challenged in some way which is why idle hands are said to be the devil's playground. I realized once that my own pattern of smoking weed was connected to wanting to make the moment more complicated, as I did with writing this book, sharing these theories and everything else in my life too. How we do anything is how we do everything so notice how you fill the spaces in your life and the stories that go with them; decide how they're serving you and choose to intentionally focus your energies onto what will better serve as you stay committed to becoming fully present.

Contentment (7) is the tipping point out of states of e-motion into a state of being present in the now where all our power exists. It is the first sign of improved health within the WEB we're weaving our life with because no longer do we need things to change in order to be content where we are when we're there. Love and INNER PEACE begins here, in the heart centre instead of the mind which can only lead us back onto the downward spiral we've spent so much time in before now. Celebrate your victory without creating a story about it, if you can help it, for doing so will take you back into the mind trap of the not-now.

Hopefulness (6) is the feeling of having hope for something better than that which has already shown up in our reality. Doubt is present due to our uncertainty that what we hope for is possible, for us, but we must back our hope with action and stay in the pre-sent moment.

Optimism (5) is hopefulness mixed with greater confidence that success is possible and we are worth the effort required to bring it into existence. It is high enough in the highrise to have risen above many of the buildings around it so more is visible from this point of view, including solutions to problems that arise as we move through life. Optimists remember that once we identify the problem we can find the solution, which my Dad reminds me is always nearby if we're open to find it; dare to look within to find the overflowing reserves of energy available to support us in the pursuit of a worthy goal or ideal.

Positive Expectation and Belief (4) is based on intentionally directed thought that gains momentum and feels real because of how much energy the idea has gained. This is where trust is formed and has been diverted to external authorities for far too long; now it is time for us to call our power back to our cells to rise above the tyranny of BS that harms more than it helps.

Enthusiasm (3) is an intense and eager enjoyment, interest or approval of something or someone that we offer our energetic TEEAM resources in support of. It's the feeling of excitement that bubbles up from within and is part of feeling truly PEACEFULL.

Passion (2) is an experience of pre-sense that gives us cause to be excited even before we can see evidence of cause to be. It makes us feel alive and has the power to move us; PEACE begins here.

Joy, Knowledge*, Empowerment, Freedom and Love (1) are the pinnacle states of being fully present where we are without need for anything to change in order for us to be ok where we are. Here we embrace the joy of the JOurneY that helped us cast our vote to be of the greatest and highest service to all the cells within and the larger ecosystem we live in too. Contribution to others can be a great way to reach higher states of being present, so long as we are not giving for the sake of getting something in return; giving without need for return allows us to fill the well within because we're able to give from our overflow instead of the reserve supply whereas giving out of obligation or expectation often means sacrificing something we need which is an irresponsible investment we generally pay for later. Giving is a sacred act and is why forgiveness is such a fundamental part of calling our power back to the present where the flow is unlimited because all time is happening now. Practicing calling your attention back to the moment you're in takes the pressure off to be other than you are which is liberating and helps to ingrain a new pattern in your self-worth, esteem and belief.

*While knowledge is highly prized in this world and was ranked as a pinnacle experience within the Emotional Guidance System, I believe it's important to consider the biblical story (myth) of the garden of Eden which said there were two trees for Eve to choose from; one was the tree of knowledge and the other was the tree of life. She was deceived because she didn't know the difference and ate from the tree of knowledge but Adam was then tempted by his woman to join her in the know-ledge she had gained by becoming conscious instead of living in the heart where conscience prevails; he got the "Adam's apple" because he knew better and did it anyway just like the ones upholding the lie now trying to hide behind suits are doing.

None of us were around at the time this story was said to have taken place so it's hearsay (information received from other people that one cannot adequately substantiate) which would not be admissible in a court of LAW but it's noteworthy because the mind can become like a mine field set and used by the devil and his agents who act on be-half of the not-now. Pay attention to the fact that all charges within the corrupted courts reflect not-now moments that either already happened or are presumed to have been premeditated in a future that doesn't exist; the not-now is a mental construct and trap used by those trained to use time and space to their advantage, at the expense of one who doesn't recognize the difference. Be aware to beware the trap.

Once something has happened or is no longer living it is no longer flexible or able to expand to reflect the potential it could have if another effort or attempt were made. It enters a contracted form that is limited by what did or didn't happen or was or wasn't included. Recorded knowledge is bound by constraints of the author's perspective or the influences behind the point of view portrayed by the one writing the story and if there are any hidden or covert agendas behind the featured event or tale being shared we need to be aware to beware.

Culturally we've been taught to give respect to credible information and sources without recognizing the hypocrisy of this notion given the subjective nature of life or the agendas of the ones approving or denying implied facts; for example, have we paid enough mind to who is paying the fact checkers of information in the public domain during the con video game? Or to the sponsors behind the alleged safety measures being imposed by the same corps' profiting from their use? It's insanity to blindly trust entities to have our best interest at heart when an entity is lifeless and lacks heart generally.

Knowledge that is written can be peer reviewed, critiqued, studied and supported by others with an interest in that area but theories only change lives once we've lived them and have real world experience to ground them with. Like when I started out this book and had lots of theoretical information I thought could help people without the lived experience to back it up it didn't feel as real as I felt it needed to be. After the five years it took for me to finally fully commit to walking my talk and living the principles I'd acquired and wanted to share, I was able to pull it all together in a month because I've used the information in practical ways so offer my story instead of a heady theory that feels ungrounded. That's the difference between knoxis (knowledge) and praxis (practice) and the journey living these theories took me on which I hope helps you to maneuver your journey more gracefully than I did.

The conscious mind is the rational mind that processes information to decide where to file it within the subconscious 'filing cabinet' mind that stores all the information with an emotional charge behind it within our inner-net. The more frequently we invest our TEEAM into an idea the more energy it accumulates and the bigger its file becomes within the subconscious and the more 'second nature' the associated pattern of thinking will become.

Emotions are subconscious patterns we attach stories and consciousness to which is why we must now do our best to separate the stories from the emotions that arise with them.

Significant Emotional Events (SEEs) stir the depths of our soul to bring up all the energies we suppressed, repressed, compressed, denied or rejected in the past because whether we like to admit it or not the barrels we tried to confine them to leak and pollute our INNER world over time. States of e-motion require we face the energies we failed to deal with or heal from in the past, like toxic barrels within the ocean of our emotions that just want to flow. While our toxic load may have a high threshold before problems surface and dis-ease (cellular disharmony within the body) appears, keeping this Highrise in mind will help you see that the energies showing up for you are trying to help you grow instead of show you're F*ed Up, Insecure, Negative/Neurotic/Needy and Emotional (AKA FINE).

While my offering of words will not necessarily change your life until you live the concepts that resonate for you and then have tales to share of your own, it's important to note that trusting theories you've never applied keeps you in your head and out of your heart.

Use information like a buffet and choose the ideas that resonate most for you to try out in your own life before trying to propagate these concepts to others who may be confused without a practical example to relate to. Recognize that our feelings are a great tool for interpreting the information the energies in motion show up to re-mind us of as an unconscious attempt to keep us out of the present where our power to choose exists.

Better Than A Movie – Moving FEAR FAR Away   22

Movies are a great way to move emotion vicariously through man-u-scripts wrote by men and women intent on capturing our Time, Energy, Effort, Attention and Money so we can sit captive to a screen that's been filled with scenes created by others that pull at our heart strings. We watch men and women acting on 'the big screen' and idolize those we see frequently because celebrities have become the modern-day gladiators, false idols and gods we revere but that's only because we've forgot the power of the mental pictures we are creating our own lives from.

Culturally we typically spend hours scrolling aimlessly through social media 'feeds' that make us believe others have it better or worse than us based on the pictures and videos shared and the number of likes, comments and sub(scribe)s we get from those we inter-act with in a virtual reality many value more than the real lives we're living. And in today's 'throw away culture' we have started throwing people away because we can't get over the BS that re-legion us into different camps of belonging.

Corp-orations even sell products we consume so that we don't have to create our own and encourage people to spend extra TEEAM to wear brands that market the corps(e) it re-presents, turning us into walking bill-boards that influence others who want to connect, relate and belong through the easiest way possible. We've stopped relating the brands we wear with the practice of 'branding' animals and slaves to show ownership and must start to see how we've been living on the ultimate Plantation where energy harvesting is the name of the game.

Our feelings are intuitive interpretations of the energies in motion in our midst and they have been weaponized against us to keep us disempowered. And if you've heard about the 'adrenochrome' industry that needs to go down with the souls using it to feed off innocents caught in an intricate trap of terror and illusion then you'll see why I've been through the ringer in the way I have. So I could expose the illusions like Jesus did in his time, which is not said to give myself any sense of importance beyond what I saw in my mind's eye when going through what I've come to call my messy awakening.

When waking up from the Matrix, I remember seeing the vision of a map with 'controllers' observing it from an elevated vantage point when suddenly a huge white light turned on that I knew was me and 'they' freaked out, wanting to know "who just woke up!?" They were panicked and I was in the scared side of the mother, maiden, and crone archetypes thinking I was the answer. This is where the lighthouse concept for enlightened or empowered ones stems from when I say boats get out of the way when we fall and need support but it was a humbling process to find that I had been trapped by my own self-righteousness and many no longer trusted the light (information) I shared because of how deluded they saw me to be. I don't blame them because that's what victims do and I don't choose to stay in a disempowered (scared) state now that I see how little status really means; embodiment is the name of the game I aim to live at the level of and that is where we stand on common ground as equals.

Getting myself out of the trap I walked myself into by revealing my cards too fast sucked, energetically and literally, but was valuable in retrospect because while I have no proof of my claims that I'd become a threat to the system, this book reveals secrets that expose the little man behind the curtain who has been projecting a larger than life image of himself onto the screen to be seen by others who've been deceived to believe the scene on the metaphoric cave wall that Plato's analogy first depicted and the Wizard of Oz picked up and ran with.

Shifting the focus from #metoo to #wetoo is the way we flip the script and win this play which is what life really is when we're through and get to look back at all the parts we played along the way. It's just necessary for us to decide which side of history we will act on behalf of; his-story or ours?

In fact, when I was leaving Toronto the morning I called 9-1-1 to report the system was corrupt and I needed protection because I'd been exposed as a threat to the existing system and knew the police were in on it but there had to be some good ones in position to fix the problem (I contemplated leaving this part out but include to show how crazy truth seems without context) I remember making dozens of phone calls to different people I believed needed access to the codes I was scared the world would lose if I got taken out of circulation early. I simply felt I was more significant than my status suggested and I wanted to make sure people could find one another if I wasn't there to connect the dots myself. I was still caught in the mental trap of thinking knowledge was power when I soon discovered theories could not help me out of the bind my mind had got me tied up in.

It was definitely crazy and I left many voicemails that wouldn't have made sense because information is not the solution and knowledge is not power-full until applied. We've just been taught that it is so that we fail to go within to retrieve what we came here to leave by the energetic signature we sign our lives with.

The early philosophers differentiated between knoxis (knowledge) and praxis (practice, as distinguished from theory) and at the time I 'woke up' I felt I knew more than I'd integrated and embodied within my energetic signature; you can't fill a full cup yet I felt bursting to add value when my greatest contribution was in holding space the way I did with Kayla who was another patient in the second place I got sent as a prisoner of the system; I have since come to see I needed to go in there to see the corruption firsthand, live to tell the tale and to also connect with those who had surrendered their power more readily than I.

Kayla was a beautiful soul that had been used and abused by life. She was pacing the hall in a boot cast while I was 'playing the game' as a bishop (chess reference) where I would only leave my room on my own terms which I did a few times with further crazy tales to share.

My approach had been inspired by the story of King David from the BIBLE I'd been told the day before. David was said to be God's favourite son who was supposed to be away when he decided to stay home and saw a woman sun bathing who he decided he wanted for himself. He'd found out who her husband was and had him sent to the frontlines to be killed so he could assume her as his bride, and so it was that I'd made up my mind to play the game as a bishop or king instead of a pawn, forgetting the castle (rook), knight and queen which all have more options than the ones I'd ironically remembered. Poignant for the position I found myself in.

When Kayla was walking by at one point I came to the doorway of my room and called her to sit with me. She sat to my right at the edge of my doorway and I asked her questions I genuinely cared to hear her answers to which I imagine started with asking why she was bruised and battered. She told me she'd become a prostitute to support herself and her brother and was worried about him because her controllers were ruthless and knew how much she loved him so could use him to get to her. It was a nightmare story to hear, let alone live through. Let us send love her way!

Acting on my intuition at one point I told her to get up, despite the boot cast she was wearing, and sit to the left of me. Why this is significant is because she had LOVE and FEAR tattooed on her knuckles and while I'd been holding her LOVE hand on my right side now I was holding her FEAR hand to my left. As we spoke I took the moonstone ring a friend had given me while in England and placed it on her finger, noticing after I'd done it that the ring covered the E moving FEAR FAR away. It was profound, especially the next year when I heard Sandra Bullock being interviewed on the Ellen show talking about her youthful looks and the fact one of the ingredients of her skincare regime was the foreskin of baby boys; which she quickly smoothed over by saying it had come from children "in a land far, far away" as if that made it any less painful to the child whose genitals were mutilated to produce it.

It's shocking to me how so many little boys get circumcised in the name of hygiene when I believe the sinister reason underlying it is that traumatized people are easier to control because we store so much fear and unprocessed energy in motion within our bodies when we're hurt; especially when our loved ones volunteer us to be sacrificed in the name of "?" – words escape me because the justifications used are outdated and irrelevant to the world we are now called to bring into being. This practice itself is actually said to be symbolic for the legal fiction and rendering of our God given name with the legal (Roman) name, according to 'Dan the Christian Man' but I am not the expert to speak into that any further. I just believe we need to see that genital mutilation of children or adults, whether through circumcision of the penis or vagina, is unnecessary trauma we have been brainwashed to believe serves a higher purpose. It does, just not the ones that are popularly considered or culturally promoted.

The truth is truly stranger than fiction and we have to start looking at the long term implications of causing harm, loss or fraud to one another, especially in the name of re-legion that thrives on sacrifice whether that be human or animal. Killing or harming another life form for the sake of gaining acceptance into or maintaining membership to a death cult-u-re means always being on edge, needing to 'do/be/have more' to remain or maintain member-ship.

Why not just be part of a cultural revolution that supports life instead? What if instead of doing what we've always done to get more of what we've always got we chose to sit with the discomfort of emotions we don't know how to face alone? How can we offer that gift to one another without causing more harm by triggering their nervous system to feel unsafe and shut down as a result?

I believe the answer is in learning to hold space for one another without trying to fill it with solutions (information) we think will work for them to solve their problems when what they really need is to feel safe enough to become resourceful and find the answers within.

That is what coaching is truly meant to be, it's just we've created an industry around offering solutions and merged coaching with mentorship, training, counselling, therapy and theories that suggest we are empty vessels that need to be filled with knowledge. What we really need is to learn how to sit in the discomfort of one another's organic unfoldment without trying to impose our Belief Systems onto one another.

Instead of looking outside of ourselves for solutions, especially when we're paying a professional to help us, we've got to learn the art of presence and bringing forth the gifts we came here to share with the world instead of hoping someone will tell us what to do. But building a stronger WEB within is necessary in order for us to learn to trust ourselves enough to hear and adhere to the in-sights from within so trusting the Universe to give us what we need instead of what we think we want is key.

Instead of turning on the 'tell a vision' while we Net-fucks and chill with someone looking to escape themselves for the sake of temporary pleasure, what if we actually practiced stillness and sitting with our highest self? What if we dared to actually retrieve the vision from within that only we can see and then remain quiet enough to hear what feels like the best next step forward?

What if we didn't need to know it all at all? What if we only needed space to hear the still small voice within that offers us the courage to try again tomorrow?

The Con Of Freedom, Fabians, Entities & My Crazy Journey To Clarity

23

Since the con video game kicked off in full gear we've lost sight of who the common enemy is and in the process we have turned on one another and our cells, calling some sheeple and others warriors, and many other names in between. But what if the truth is that our common hue is only one aspect of the man-i-tie my identity to and we're being called to untie our self-image from all the labels, statuses, titles and entities we've been trained to believe make us any more or less than anyone else?

What if we started to see how the pretend self is the mask we were wearing before de facto governmental bodies tried to impose unhealthy mandates onto people who complied because we've been lied to about who has our best interest at heart?

What if we started to see the core identity underneath the image we felt safe enough to show the world (our pretend identity) was actually our sacred (empowered) self who remains ever-connected to the sacred nature of the Universe? And what if we started to see the Uni-verse as the one song we are all singing along to?

When we start to see that our power stance is in the questions we are willing to ask and the space we are willing to hold for the answers to be shared, we can take the pressure off ourselves to have it all together or seem to have life figured out. In a court of law, questions are more powerful than answers that a trained man or woman can ask details about that would make it seem our word was not our bond the way we can claim it is and then stick with. Opponents will always try to knock us off balance by sending us into a not-now moment where the legal fiction lives but questions are how we get back to the moment where all power lives.

I remember when I heard the call to become a life coach after switching programs in University without a clue what to do with an English degree if becoming a teacher wasn't my goal. When I discovered the term 'life coach' I felt the resonance of truth and purpose within the role and knew that it was for me, but my age and inexperience made me feel ill-equipped to fulfill that call. And when I received higher guidance that said I could smoke (weed) or coach but I couldn't do both, I punished myself for choosing to continue a habit I knew wasn't (good) for me by not packaging my services in a way that could truly serve. As a result I just gave away all that I invested a lot of TEEAM to learn and experience and I failed to package my goods in packages people could purchase and work their way through in a structured way. This book is proof of the change in me this process has helped me come to; I hope my honesty and transparency is helping you to take the masks off and be more real too.

I devalued myself and what I had to offer because I was acting against my higher wisdom willingly and share this now because it's precisely what the con video game requires players to do in order to steal our power.

Each time we dawn a mask because an outer authority figure told us "we have to" we automatically place ourselves in the dysfunctional creative spectrum of obligation and irresponsibility; the functional alternative is constraint and freedom, but even that we must now consider from a deeper level.

Freedom is an externally based experience we either have or don't have. It can be taken away or given to us, by choice or force, in the domain we are in; in a virtually based reality this is literally the www. url(d) within the public domain of the internet where the one who owns the domain also gets to censor what is shown there, how it is presented and how engagement is rewarded or condemned. Free-dom is an illusion.

Being free, on the other hand, is an experience that we feel; it is a verb used to describe an action, state or occurrence that predicates something in the sentence. Which is where we have to start looking deeper into the words themselves and why lawyers are required to 'article' upon graduation for a period of time.

Article: any of a small set of words or affixes (such as *a, an*, and *the*) used with nouns to limit or give definiteness to the application, or, a member of a particular or distinctive kind or class of things.

This process is so taxing to the man or woman acting as a devil's advocate to win the game they are forced to release all shame for their actions as a professional in the name of winning at all costs. This is also where the cream of the crop rise to the top and 'secret societies' choose their next board (bored) members, like the Fabian Society does, which uses the symbol of the 'Wolf in Sheep's Clothing' that I inadvertently mentioned in the crazy tale I wrote without knowing the covert connection I was making.

According to the Macmillan Dictionary of Historical Terms the Fabian Society is named after the Roman general Quintus Fabius Maximus who employed delay tactics against his enemy to drain them of energy and resources to avoid pitched battle but secure victory nonetheless. "The name is meant to imply the rejection of revolutionary methods and the belief that universal suffrage will eventually result in socialism after a process of educational and legislative advance... the Fabian Society's aim of reorganizing society 'by the emancipation of land and capital from individual and class ownership, and the vesting of them in the community for the general benefit" is a dangerous proposition to and for us all. For this reason the Fabian Society is a supporting pillar of the WHO's edict "you'll own nothing and be happy" with what we're given back from what legal criminals would otherwise steal from us, with our consent, if we fail to stand up now.

Edict: "An official order or proclamation issued by a person in authority; it is a decree, order, command, commandment, mandate or proclamation."

I come from farmers and understand the power of planting seeds,

I've just been learning how to plant seeds of hope in the hearts of men and women who are called to re-member we are the ones who empower the corps(e) and the ones working on its be-half who will also suffer if we don't choose to do the right thing and call ourselves to account for our choices as men and women to uphold mandates that cause harm on all levels.

It is time for us to call for liability, accountability and personal responsibility for acting honourably and in good faith which means in a way we are able to honour and respect ourselves for the choices we have made to impact ourselves and those around us.

We've been duped (deceived) to believe we must live at the effect end of the cause and effect equation which is where we flip out of the functional creative spectrum into the dysfunctional reactive spectrum, based on the orders of the edicts we follow and who we allow to call the shots in our lives; this statement has taken on a far too literal meaning since the new program was unleashed in the silent war between the public and private which we will be used as pawns in until we stop letting ourselves be overtaken. This war is called a 'mixed war' that mixes us up and colours us according to laws made by men that have corrupted and converted us to think instead of feel.

A mixed war is one which is made on one side by public authority, and on the other by mere private persons/citizens/slaves owned by the state; the alter-native is to be natives and originals which mean standing as men and women, as was intended.

Earlier I'd mentioned 'The Matrix' is a documentary because predictive programming requires that the rules of the game be revealed in order for the controllers to remain in honour. But what I've experienced with the implied charge against me for speaking in public without having previously declared my claim of right to remain in my private capacity with all common law (unwritten and unlimited) rights reserved at all times as a woman is that rules can and will be applied to us until we say no more and hold the professional accountable as men and women causing harm to fellow men and women. What the legal professionals haven't wanted us to know is that we can correct any mistakes by lawful notice once we're aware of the true rules of the game and how we've been converted into something less than we truly are, so long as we cause no harm and keep the peace. Fraud, such as the professionals are upholding, is a threat to the wellbeing of all life and must now be called out and corrected by each of us. There is great power in numbers when our emotions are in check and we can create instead of react.

Getting locked up in 2019 for reporting the truth to the authority figures I thought were supposed to protect and defend the public from criminals I had come to see were no different from the criminal rings I was trained to believe they fought against, I soon learned the biggest difference lays in the legalities and jurisdictions where everything is relative; juris-diction determines who gets to apply their rules to the players of the game so until we claim the right to be lawfully (not legally) self-governing we are subject to the implied laws of the implied govern-mental bodies we must pay mind to and every election we vote in gives them authority over us who agree to be represented by one who can speak for those under their riding.

The men who agreed I needed a psychological evaluation that day were protecting and defending the corporation they pledged an oath of allegiance to; I didn't believe I was causing anyone harm but I was telling an inconvenient truth that was dangerous to me and my family but it took me until now to see their hands were tied while the lies still ruled the roost.

I hadn't even considered the Mental Health Act to be a threat back then but given all I went through with a sound mind and pure heart, though tainted by FEAR and lower level emotions that put me on the defensive, I got to see a manhole hidden directly in front of all who see the open secret the system and its legions are committed to defending.

After experiencing how the professionals turn the tribe against the individual to isolate and influence its prisoners firsthand I had a lot of resentment, resistance and regret to get over in the years since that turning point call that I'm glad I made when I did for all it revealed and forced me to heal before the insanity went public.

Were it not for that experience I would have been far more trusting of the professionals than I now am, or even joined their leagues as my training had all prepared me to do.

We must be mindful that not all realize the harm their compliance and need for controlled emotions is causing healthy and free men and women who feel trapped by the lies. So we must be full of care around those paid to deceive unsuspecting souls to believe lies their in-doctor-nation brain-washed them to buy hook, line and sinker. And we must be especially care-full around those so used to committing fraud against men and women converted into lesser things by the tricks of their trade that they'll try to move false claims forward with impunity like the man trying to convict my person of an implied violation of the 'Reopening Ontario Act' which was unlawfully evoked by a de facto government who have overstepped their jurisdiction, knowing the men and women acting on the corps' behalf are who will pay karmically when the masses discover the rules I'm doing my best to lay out for you here.

In the implied violation that called me back to life, the man current-lie acting against me (and every other man or woman involved in this trespass on my rights) have shown themselves to be acting in 'bad faith' which is a legal term generally defined by the Supreme Court of Canada as "conduct involving 'malicious intent' or that 'exceeds the limits of discretion reasonably exercised'" that is evaluated on a case by case basis.

In contrast, 'good faith' is defined as "honesty or sincerity of intention" and in a legal context means "that parties must not lie or otherwise knowingly mislead each other about matters directly linked to the performance of the contract." Which is where our cultural propensity toward 'pro-social lies' (lies intended to benefit others) has systematically destroyed our faith in one another, starting with myths like Santa Claus, the Easter Bunny, Tooth Fairy and the BIBLE as mythical examples we sell the younge to acclimatize them to a culture that promotes lies the higher we climb the ladder we're taught gives us power.

Every lie gets exposed eventually and while we've cult-u-rally encouraged some lies, often referred to as 'white lies' for the sake of 'innocent fun' we believe won't cause much harm, it's time for us to recognize that a half truth is a full lie that destroys faith and trust we can no longer afford to tell. We need to read the fine print before committing ourselves to contract with entities that will 'hold us to it' if we don't know 'The Santa Clause.' Tim Allen's movie by that same name actually offers viewers a secret that most overlook because we aren't common-lie told black magic only works if the rules are made available in plain sight; that way those causing another harm can use the excuse of plausible deniability to say they acted in 'good faith' by warning the public without also informing them that no contract is binding if one of the signing parties are not fully aware of the details.

The man acting as prosecutor in the implied charge against me pledged his allegiance to the BAR association nearly three decades ago and is a professional bully knowingly trying to cause harm, loss and fraud against me and the others who 'got nailed' for speaking at the same event in 2021, except I am the only woman remaining standing because the others all hired representatives to handle their affairs for them. I tried to help others understand how doing so made them 'wards of the court' who are deemed incompetent to speak for themselves which is an experience I experienced and will not surrender myself willingly to again but the method I am using is untried and untested so I did not push it or try to change any minds. My own testimony will speak for itself on October 31, 2022 when I stand for myself, fully present as a woman in my private capacity with all common law rights reserved at all times as my lawful notices have already proclaimed without acknowledgement (which means they were accepted).

To proclaim something is to declare what one considers important with due emphasis publicly but given the private nature of the implied-to-be-public court system we will see how deep the lies go as they try to hang me at every turn; hence it being called a trial where the legal beagles 'try all' to nail men and women to the metaphoric cross where their pre-charge life stops and their new life with a new label would begin.

It's clear to see how corrupted this system is yet it's the equivalent of David facing off against Goliath when a man or woman goes up against the men and women acting on be-half of a corps(e) that are true-lie boxes on top of boxes designed to confine real people to smaller and smaller spaces we've been trained to believe we need to pay for ahead of time in the death cult that has led us to early graves. Yet this is precisely why I am grateful to my younger self for leading us into that experience in 2019 and then for accepting the call to attend a small-town rally where I've been called to be myself fully without limitation; this is the difference between contracts with entities that limit us to what was written and agreements between people who can change the terms based in a world where our word is our bond because we live in honour.

The legal beagles working for the devil don't want the general public to know this because they always set up loop holes the elite know to jump over that are set up to be traps for the unsuspecting. It's time for us to stop trying to screw one another for our own benefit (profit) at the expense of the other (people) and be part of a cultural turn around.

I suspect (have an idea or impression of the existence, presence, or truth of something without certain proof) my lawful notices were not responded to in hopes I'm listening to advice from some guru and can be tripped up in court by a seasoned professional but what the pros didn't expect was to meet a quick-study like me so fully committed to being my true self despite the odds that I'm all in and not afraid to tell the truth even when it makes me look bad, plus I've got good people in my corner who care because they see the power of one too.

Few have faced the ugly truth the way I have and healed the hurt to see it for what it is.

I'll always remember my second day and night as a prisoner of the mental health system, having been sent to the 10th floor of Hamilton's St. Joseph's Hospital which was a nightmare experience that I am fortunate to have got to leave after only one night, but only because

I have an eye for details and I believe my presence there limited the professionals' ability to act freely with the others in their grips.

In Simcoe General Hospital where I was initially taken and held in a cell in the emergency room overnight with an unlocked door so I could use the shared facilities, I was actually having quite a lot of fun because they knew I was not a threat to anyone and had simply been too loose with my words in a society based on lies that tries to confine truthtellers to the fringes of society. A friend came to visit me and brought pizza and tea unsure as to why I was in there so we went live on Facebook for some real talk of an uncommon variety. It's embarrassing to rewatch because I was ungrounded but not overly different from my normal state as one who dares to think and live outside of the box. One of the men acting as Doctors had later told me to give him my phone, typed in Stanislav Grof's name and told me to read all about him and his work.

I'd been open about the fact I'd done 8 DMT ceremonies with a Shaman earlier that year plus a few other psychedelic experiences in order to get the breakthrough I was going through at that time and knew of Grof's "Holotropic Breathwork therapy" so presumed the man had documented his suspicion in my file. In retrospect I suspect not. I'd got to connect with other patients and staff who benefitted from my presence in that place that night and have stories to tell for another time but I had no idea what was coming for me next and I doubt the staff there had any clue either.

The next day a girl from the grade below me in public school acted as the ambulance driver to Hamilton with two of her colleagues. I was having fun with them and still riding the magic of the moment presuming they would do some brain scans and tests to see what was going on but that's not really how it works.

When the three of them wheeled me up to the 10th floor and I saw the energy pattern of this new place I realized the game had just changed and child's play was no longer the way forward. I was alarmed and we'd been having fun together so they asked if they could stay with me for a few minutes to help me settle in but were told they needed to leave immediately. It was intense and I don't know what the experience was like in that moment for them but things got real for me real quick.

Intimidation and denial of a patient's dignity and equality is how people are converted into patients in that place and the professionals are trained to do it well. It's insane, truly, whereas the ones in there need presence and compassionate connection to come back to the present where they can actually use their power. It's heartbreaking to see and devastating to experience firsthand which is why so few people actually talk about their experiences or the systemic abuse that takes place behind closed doors. Except I believe I got sent there to reveal the experience I had to heal from, in the years since and know many others need support to do too, but not from the same trained professionals who purposefully avoided eye contact with patients to dehumanize us and make us feel insignificant. Fortunately, it didn't work and I saw straight through it because all my training helped me recognize the unspoken cues that were meant to create an emotional response that would lead to a reward of medication to placate and dull down the one terrorized by those entrusted to their care. This is the cue-response-reward training method used to domesticate animals and people alike.

The two plus weeks beyond this second day and night in the system which I spent in the Mood Disorders Program up the mountain in Hamilton, where I was sent to next, were memorable in their own way too but why this part of the story is significant is that I realized the moment I was wheeled in that second place it was dangerous for the soul, heart, body and mind. So I took the time to review the two pieces of paper I'd been handed that were responsible for my detention and at the bottom of the second page it says "You have the right to retain and instruct a lawyer without delay" except that was not the experience I had and why I have handled my affairs regarding the summons issued for my person (with knowledge of Event 201's strategy in mind) differently than those also selected for the real life equivalent of Hunger Games.

I was denied the right to speak to a lawyer without a psychiatrist's permission once I realized the precarious situation I was in and requested to exercise this right; I realize this is not common knowledge to those outside the system because we generally don't know the deal until we need to and by then it's too late.

Because I'd incorporated my own business, travelled quite a bit and went through two visa application processes while dating an Englishman, I knew that the full name and address need to match and noticed the number of the road had been missed out on the first form; it was addressed to my Grandparents' when my government ID was still registered to my Dad's next door. Were it not for that detail I wouldn't have contested the first form I was issued but some part of me was terrified of getting lost in the system so I demanded it be corrected. When I received a second form having spelled out the required changes for them, my middle names had been removed, as had the postal code. I was alarmed, especially because that second place employed so many evil tactics that I followed my inner guidance to demand that second form be corrected before I was transferred to the next place (which I didn't have any idea where that would be) and was told "it won't matter where you're going" by a woman who seemed to enjoy the power her position gave her.

This was the same woman who had come into my room to chastise me for something and then walked out, closing my door behind her to make it appear I was locked in. I had walked over, pulled it open slightly to show I wasn't going to give them the response they were looking for, and went back to writing in my journal on the mattress on the floor in my cell. She was toying with me like a cat with a mouse.

What I experienced under the Mental Health Act was nothing short of terrorism which is "the unlawful use of violence and intimidation, especially against civilians, in the pursuit of political aims." While the violence I experienced was not physical the line is fine when already uncertain of where you stand socially or physically if you don't know where you're being taken and this kind of threat is issued.

I accept this sounds like a crazy story, and believe me it was, but I will stand, affirm and testify to its truth in any court of competent jurisdiction (common law) with men and women willing to recognize the repeating of history we're experiencing now where Martin

Niemöller's poem *First They Came* is more relevant than most can bear to believe.

More or less it goes like this: First they came for 'those ones' and I didn't speak out because I wasn't one of them. Then they came for 'these ones' and I didn't speak out because I wasn't one of them either. Then they came closer to home, rounding up my neighbours, and I got nervous but still didn't speak out because I didn't want to upset anyone who might turn on me, but then when they did come for me, as was only a matter of time in retrospect, there was no one left to speak out for me and his-story tells our dread-full fate.

When I got out weeks later I contacted a lawyer many in my extended family have used and told her my traumatized story of the horrors I'd experienced at the hands of the system. She met with me, listened compassionately and suggested I get some counselling or therapy to process all I'd been through and believed about the world she knew secrets about that she wasn't allowed to speak aloud. Her response suggested she believed me but it wasn't a case she was willing to take on; she didn't charge me for her time that day and I was grateful for that extension of kindness after all I had been through. I didn't understand why at that time but now see that her hands were tied by the same system that had tried to convert me into an addict and dependent every step of the way.

If I added that the psychiatrist in the Moods Disorders program met with me for the longest amount of time I'd got to see him the whole two+ weeks I was locked up given his role was primarily to diagnose and treat with pre-script(ion)s his patients must live with the consequences of, you might be surprised by his personal guarantee.

I'd been told I couldn't leave for two weeks after I was shipped there on the third day of my institutionalization experience, after my form 1 had allegedly been flipped into a form 3 which was a two week involuntary hold; I never received a copy of this form which is fraudulent, but I lived and learned and now know better.

After experiencing the 'possum effect' on my third day there when the energy vampirism terrified me to the point of passing out in front of one of the nurses after I'd been forced to do an anal swab I was pretty sure was for the sake of the ones I suspected were keen to rape me, I realized I needed to show some level of compliance or feared they might take matters into their own hands against my will. You might be surprised to note that when I 'came to' on the floor of the living room across from the nurse's station shortly after, having spilled the water that I'd been holding, I picked myself and my empty foam cup up off the floor, avoided eye contact and walked myself swiftly back to my room and no one mentioned a thing about it; I would have thought a medical professional would have insisted I be checked out after such an occurrence as I am quite sure it was observed, but no. I thought that to be one of many strange events while there.

Knowing that would be used as evidence to reinforce the box on the form checked "shown or are showing a lack of competence to care for yourself" I decided to agree to take the anti-psychotic medication the man acting as my Psychiatrist wanted to put me on, but I advocated for the lowest dose possible. A Pharmacist I know confirmed the prescription issued shouldn't impair my cognitive abilities too much and so it was that I allowed my system to be poisoned on their orders until the evening before I was released when I asked a nurse in passing "any chance you know when I might be able to get out of here?" and she said my name was 'in red on the board' which meant they could no longer detain me without my consent.

I'm a Thanksgiving baby so I spent my 32nd birthday locked up and they were vague about when I was able to leave due to staffing issues over the holiday, they said. I didn't push because when your every move is evaluated in a system that wants to eliminate any sign of radical or emotionally-charged behaviour you must walk lightly. But the moment it was confirmed I could leave I declined the drugs I'd never wished to have in my system in the first place and the next day when I'd arranged for friends to pick me up, the Psychiatrist tried to get me to stay and told me I'd be leaving against Doctor's orders which meant no follow-up support from the system that had revealed so much about the cultural sickness of the world at present. He also personally guaranteed me that I would fail to self-regulate and when

I did I should go to the Emergency Room, saying too much sleep would make me depressed and too little sleep would make me manic. That was the best advice I received throughout that whole experience because healthy self-regulation truly is the safest way forward.

Two weeks later I did get my Mom to take me to Emerge when I no longer wanted to live having publicly humiliated myself with Facebook live videos of the messy awakening process I'd went through while writing a book about INNER PEACE I clearly didn't have at the time, not to mention the covert bullying I'd experienced at the hands of professionals I no longer respected nor wanted to join the ranks of as I'd trained to be able to do, and all the other ways my former self-image got destroyed in that process led me to another level of unveiling my authentic self.

As you can imagine, I could go on about these experiences or the rock bottom I hit months later that only the Universe could have orchestrated, which led me to a Crisis Stabilization Bed program for 5 days to confirm my hunch that the mental health system is a trap, but it's time to focus on what is presently in front of us which brings me back to the legal system and the false claim against my person which I now know isn't me.

Recently I sat with my Papa to watch the movie *1917* about a protagonist (main character) who was ordered to deliver an order to the Colonel in command of a legion of soldiers set to walk straight into a trap set by the opposing side. There is a scene where an officer says 'the only way this war ends: last man standing' but given all I've been through and witnessed as a woman with a unique relationship with words, I've come to see that we've been missing the point this whole time in a subtle but significant way.

A soldier is a role filled by a man or woman whose identity gets converted into that which he or she is acting as therefore while the man acting as a soldier still thinks of himself as a man, his position takes precedence and he is forced to cause harm and loss to others on behalf of the legion he is pledged to. This is why fraternities and sororities call new members 'a pledge' who have accepted a bid to join but have not yet been initiated. And when corporations or entrepreneurs 'bid on a job' we unintentionally use the same language with different implications and outcomes.

Remember that in a court of multiple jurisdictions, laws are set based on precedents where past decisions are considered as authority for deciding subsequent cases involving identical or similar facts, or similar legal issues. Like the Meads vs Meads case law precedent passed in 2012 that converts any man or woman who does not know how to maintain standing in their private capacity with all common law rights reserved at all times into a status that draws them into the public domain with limited liability for the men and women acting on behalf of the (corrupted) crown to prosecute them which means to "institute legal proceedings against (a person or organization) or to continue with (a course of action) with a view to its completion."

Prosecute is similar to persecute which is to "subject (someone) to hostility and ill-treatment, especially because of their race or political or religious beliefs" which could be seen as a coincidence if the covert deception and corruption were not hopefully becoming clear.

Returning to the infamous notion that 'last man standing' is the only way to win a war, we've got to see that the man's position supersedes the truth of who he is until he reclaims the right to be himself and live by the unwritten and unlimited common law tenants to keep the peace which means cause no harm, loss or fraud to another. Just like freedom is not the same as being free, what we've been taught to fight for is the very thing that can be taken away if we haven't owned it within our cells.

We've been deceived by the legalese and jargon that applies multiple meanings to the same words in order to confuse those who believe they understand the meaning of the word without also comprehending the implied meanings being agreed to simultaneously.

There are significant karmic consequences to acting on behalf of corporations that steal Time, Energy, Effort, Attention, Money in the name of being on a team going nowhere because they fail to see we are now here and it's time to acknowledge the gaps (in awareness) we've been overlooking within ourselves and society, lest we continue to fall into them.

Before we get into the karmic implications of acting on be-half of a corrupted corps(e) it's necessary to recognize that the Latin root word 'corpus' means 'body' with corporeal and corporal being distinct derivatives designed to confuse and lose the majority; any good sales training will reaffirm that if you confuse them you lose them because people naturally gravitate toward certainty. Recognize how the brightest lights have been deployed into the darkest places to be dulled down and snuffed out in a spiritual war we didn't know we were born into and are here to win together as originals.

While 'corporeal' means "having, consisting of, or relating to a physical material body," according to Merriam-Webster within legal contexts "corporeal moves beyond the body to describe things (such as property and money) that exist in the same physical realm that the body exists in, as opposed to the nonphysical realm of reputations and well-being and the like." Corporeal thus applies to the legal definition of a person which can be used to describe a man or woman, or a corporate entity, which we don't realize until we have seasoned eyes to see the lies and call for li(e)ability of the one lying.

A corporation is also known as 'body corporate' which is an organization or group (of persons) that is identified by a particular name and that acts as an entity.

An entity is a thing with distinct and independent existence denoted with a proper name which can be a corporate name or abstract thought form that accrues energy because we give it our power. What isn't commonly talked about is how each substance has an entity those using it are subject to which relates to both drugs and alcohol, whether prescribed or of a street variety. This war of terrorism needs to stop and community is the key which is why ours have been and are being systematically (and systemically) destroyed.

Systemically: in a way that relates to or affects the whole of something.

Systematically: according to a fixed plan or system; methodically.

Another significant term to be aware of is menticide: a systematic effort to undermine and destroy a person's values and beliefs, as by the use of prolonged interrogation, drugs, torture, etc., and to induce radically different ideas in those who see the world differently than the way the corps(e) wishes us to see it. This was exactly what I experienced within the mental health system and blamed the ones in control for when they were just being used as pawns by evil they felt trapped by too.

I'll always remember when I was wheeled into the 10th floor of Hamilton's psych ward where the reversed roles of the prisoners and guards was made clear to me on an energetic level. I'd never experienced anything quite like it but did remember hearing of the pattern in a psychology class at University. I just couldn't understand how so many were willing to go along with it despite knowing how unhealthy, unnatural and not ok the evil is to follow. Yet entities have a mind of their own and they overtake the ones who become subject to them.

The suicide entity is one such thought form that grips those who wake up to the corruption but feel trapped by it with nowhere to turn. It's why, according to *Choices Psychotherapy* medical doctors, dentists, police officers, veterinarians, financial services, real estate agents, electricians, lawyers, farmers and pharmacists are the jobs with the highest suicide rates; people serving in these positions had to put out a lot of TEEAM in order to get the position before finding out just how soul destroying it is. And because so many feel the pressure to pay back all that went into getting the title, plus then what's required to rebuild our identity after, it all just feels like too much. The suicide entity knows how to reinforce all of this limiting BS and for too long it has taken too many of us out of circulation early.

In 2018-19 when I was in limbo with getting this book done or knowing how to genuinely contribute in this world, it gripped me too. And when the uncertainty of how things current-lie are sinks in, the entity rears its head to see if it has caught me in a weak moment where it can take advantage and call me closer to a threshold I will not cross. I comprehend the cost of crossing that line and want others to be aware of it too, especially because the legislation and bills the currently corrupted govern-mental bodies have been passing covertly during the cover of COVID-19 has made it easier than ever to be 'put down' if we don't feel like carrying on and many won't want to when they find out the ugly truth if they feel like no one cares or would miss them. We need to rebuild community now so this is not the case regardless of how close to that point we already are.

Recognize that exiting the game early means coming back into a reality where you didn't do what you're here to do now and only you can. The evil entities that live backwards know it and they're eager to help us end our lives early so we lose our chance and one opportunity to do what we came here uniquely qualified and called for.

This entity values comfort and knows every story in the book about why discomfort is dangerous because to the existing Belief Systems, within a polluted system, change for the better leads to death for it; it would rather we die than the limiting BS it's bought into. We are social creatures meant to be in community but the existing options have become toxic to its members and it's up to us to rebuild without the corporate banner.

When I went through my 'messy awakening' in 2019 I said that we need to bring together all the major religions and traditions of the world to refine their stories and concepts down to their shared values and virtues; once all were on the table we could see their commonalities and develop a Belief System that will serve us better as a collective. That's what I believe the man referred to as Jesus did by studying many of the great traditions of his time which he then lived, without an instruction manual to do so, and in so doing his words became the manual others based their BS and mystery schools on. What we must see is that what is written is limited because it stops growing once confined to the chosen words to define it; there is no breathing room in words for it is the breath that speaks them that gives them life.

It's time for us to become the authority of our own life by learning to feel truth which is the difference between states of e-motion and being; energies in motion that have unresolved memories from the past take us out of the present while pre-sense is the experience of calling our power back to the now where change always begins.

Originals Have No Status – Energy Harvesting, Magic & Human Trafficking

24

We are spiritual beings having a hue-man experience and it's time for us to add in the extra E to reflect the energy we must intentionally direct instead of let be directed for us, like the movies and videogames that so many invest their TEEAM into.

It's time for us to recognize the spiritual nature of the current war for souls we're in and consciousness is the con sent to have us buy bull instead of BS (Belief Systems) that will genuinely save our souls before we meet our maker. Which is part of what I learned first-hand from the summons my person received and I believe could be a useful perspective for you to consider now as we bring about the New Orderly World.

The Hierarchy of Creation shows the order of ownership within the Uni-verse where we're either dancing to the beat of our own drum or we're marching to someone else's orders. God is just one name applied to the energy of all that is which is the pinnacle given there is nothing that isn't energy, therefore nothing that is not of GOD; Grand Overall Designer or Great Orchestra Director are befitting acronyms for the energy of all that is, we just have to stop getting offended by the boxes applied to it that make us think we're talking about something different than all that is. All that is includes everything until man applies his own rules to that energy and calls it something other than it originally was.

The plight of 'aboriginal people' is a great example because man and woman are originals before co-opted and converted into an 'ab-original' status without realizing 'ab' is a prefix meaning 'away; from' that moves the original into a lesser standing that requires a 'status card' for identification to verify the limited benefits given to men and women converted by the legal fiction to gain jurisdiction and make (ab)originals control-able.

Once in a contracted state we're said to be subject to the rules of the one we understand, which in a corrupted court actually means you stand under their jurisdiction if you step into the trap set by the professionals we've been indoctrinated to trust.

Energy harvesting is big business because energy is all there is so to think vampirism is reserved for the movies or folklore is an illusion of illusions given Mel Gibson's correct claim that Hollywood was built on the blood of babies. A controversial claim indeed yet the current Wikipedia 'Vampire (disambiguation)' definition "is a being from folklore who subsists by feeding on the life essence of the living' which is how the film industry feeds off of us.

I remember calling a family member when I'd first been sent to the Mood Disorders Program and telling him about the energy vampirism, magic of the moment that is the true nature of life and the fact witches were just misunderstood women (and men) who were made to be scapegoats in communities that needed someone to blame for natural occurrences they couldn't explain; to say it went over like a lead balloon would be accurate. That was just way too outside of his familiar Belief System so to believe I was crazy and needed to be locked away made sense; it's a personal example of recognizing cognitive dissonance in action.

To then introduce a concept as horrible as child sacrifice, Satanic ritual and adrenochrome where DUMBS (Deep Underground Military Bases) and whole islands exist with 'inventory' under a certain age is just too extreme to be considered by most but denial only perpetuates the problem. And yes, this is hearsay given I have been fortunate to not personally witness these alleged hell-holes (praise the law'd) though I believe denied fragments of both you and I are present there because we all came to this plan-ET to return to wholeness and our denied aspects will remain in others until we call them back and reintegrate them as movement of e-motion helps us do.

In a far milder way we must even consider how the myth of Satan Claws at Christ-mass is where a familiar entity legally breaks into every home that believes the myth, to climb down the spine of the pine tree people dress up and make offerings of gifts to, at a highly commercialized time in his-story, known as the Xmas holly daze (holidays). "Conjecture" I hear a lawyer appeal which is 'an opinion or conclusion formed on the basis of incomplete information' but what is true beyond a reasonable doubt in this life anyway except lived experience?

I dare to say it is truth which can be felt when tuned into the heart of 'the field' we are all connected to and through and must re-member our inherent membership to.

Entities prey on those who pray to false idols deified and revered by innocents trained to trust others more than themselves. And in the movies we must remember that evil must be invited in, trusting innocence and naivety to leave one open to destruction.

In the story I wrote on the plane from Arizona into DC before the insanity of this world became more apparent to me, from lived experience, I wrote: "The chariot drivers we choose are thus incredibly important because when the snake shows up at your door as a beautiful distraction, the Queen must trust herself enough to see what's really happening before it's too late."

This passage is connected to the warning I heeded, delivered through my Dad's wife Bonnie, that I was about to be kidnapped by a man I didn't know but would have trusted implicitly had I not felt the resonance of truth in her words when she said them.

The five days I spent at the Hilton Embassy Suites in Arizona prior to my return home were the result of following my intuition when I was in an expanded state of awareness that was truly out of this world. I wasn't scheduled to be there as I'd flown out to Arizona for a business opportunity with the six-day first date dude I felt wanted to use me for my gifts and I wasn't game to put profits over people. So instead of following his plan, I flowed with the magick of the moment and spent two days in the guest room of a man who knew Muhhamad Ali personally before following BrainTap to the Embassy Suites where they had a booth at an Optician's conference I strolled into without even considering a ticket might be required. It's funny in retrospect because so much of that whole experience was like a movie I had a blast playing in yet I'll cut to the relevant part.

I met a married man at that conference who claimed to have been my soulmate from 11 lifetimes before and who seemed to be dialled into the realm of spirit in a way I aspired to be. I had no intentions of anything more than 'saving the world' given I arranged what I called a preliminary peace summit to be hosted in my suite with some of those who were still local from the conference I'd discovered BrainTap at which is another story for another time.

In retrospect I see that it was a combination of my ego trying to make something happen to ensure I didn't return empty handed from the second three-week sojourn I'd taken West that year to network with this same circle and also an INNER knowing that I was exactly where I was meant to be. The meeting didn't happen as planned given only my friend who'd come to Arizona for the conference came to support my initiative and dash my disappointment that things hadn't come together as planned; yet what he didn't get to experience was the real meeting that took place later that night where I won the trust of a twenty year Navy Captain who was playing with a devil character named Damien who wanted nothing to do with one who claimed to be a siren of the light with full commitment (AKA me). It was epic to say the least but I'd lost my filters and was fully walking in faith which my proclaimed soulmate took advantage of the next night while I was still flying high on my perceived win from the night before.

At the time I was seeing an Indian guy from a wealthy family who approached our relationship like a business transaction rather than a love-based dynamic. I'd went against my intuition to commit to officialising our relationship the month before but once again my loyalty had me feeling trapped in something we both knew wasn't meant to last. He'd wanted to be part of the magick I was experiencing in Arizona, while he was visiting his family in India, and I was getting frustrated by his need to be included when the magick of the moment moves too quickly to bring others at a different frequency along without having to slow down to catch them up. He and I were on a video call when the married man messaged about connecting for one reason or another and headed over to my suite; I'd wrapped up the call with my boyfriend saying something about hoping his intentions were pure and opened the door to evil of an unexpected kind.

I wanted to share the magical experiences I'd been having and the realizations I was having about how all the experiences I'd been led to over the years were tying together, including the fact that the conference taking place at the hotel after the one BrainTap was at that brought me to the 'Embassy' in the first place was an FBI/CIA conference which sounds so ridiculous it must be true! And how the bar tender with an angel's name who served me virgin prickly pears when I met some of the agents in attendance gave me his black onyx bracelet with two dogs fighting over the ring between because he had a feeling I'd be needing it more than he did; it was better than a movie script and I was caught up in the magick of it all.

I was noticing many other subtle details about the hotel itself where I'd included some of the frontend staff in the fun I was having so made allies I came to need in an unexpected way on my final day and ultimately I was carried away by it all and my sense of importance within it.

He listened and shared higher-level 'channeled' insights I was fascinated by while I showed him relevant pictures on my computer and tied all the stories I was sharing together; he made me feel like I was really special. I also hadn't been sleeping much for a few days because I was so high on the energies I'd come into in this expanded state of awareness but what happened next jarred me because I betrayed myself and my INNER code of honour.

He told me that he was guided to kiss my third eye and lips, back and forth a few times, which I was reluctant to allow given he was married and I was technically in a relationship too, but he played on the martyr archetypal energies all saviors have when in their scared side. He said it was for the benefit of the world which was the focus of the story I was pulling together for him with all the dots I thought I was connecting, and so I gave in so long as it was for 'the greater good' – you can roll your eyes and gag with me ☺. So then when he suggested a shower to clean off all the energy of being taken advantage of that I'd shared and experienced over the years, I was already under a sex-magic spell I didn't even know was a thing. And then when he said he could heal my womb by taking advantage of me under the guise of healing me, I shake my head to tell you I bought his BS hook, line and sinker and have had much energetic clearing to do for it since.

It was a novel experience I'm wiser to now and share in hopes it prevents another from being used and hood winked the way I was which means to be deceived by false appearance. And that was when things intensified even more.

I told my boyfriend the next morning what had happened and justified my actions because I didn't want to accept I'd just been duped by someone I'd quickly trusted without just cause to. And the understandable upset I caused meant hours of conversation with a betrayed Scorpion when I just wanted to be riding the magick of the moment without regard for the pain my betrayal had caused him who was travelling back to Canada at the time I told him. It wasn't good and I reached a point where I felt like Khaleesi from *Game of Thrones* who was eventually killed by her lover because she had become power hungry and stopped listening to her advisors; to ensure that wasn't my fate I created a Facebook group for men I believed would keep me true if I started to buy my own BS too much, but I already had without realizing it, and I told my crushed lover that if he wanted to discuss it anymore he'd have to do it there because I couldn't handle him on my own anymore. I used the group to escape my own consequences much like the corps(e) does and if I could do it differently I would but I was doing the best I could with the pot of energies in motion I'd stirred and wasn't managing well.

At the same time the man who taught me sex magic is real told me he had a local 'switched on' friend he wanted me to meet and made arrangements for him to come see me. I don't think I even had his contact information but he came to the hotel the day before my scheduled flight to meet me and I remember feeling like he had stuff going on under the surface he kept a pretty tight wrap on. When he told me he'd be glad to give me a ride to the airport the next day I thought it sounded great as the suite was an unexpected expense so to get a free ride to the airport was welcome but that 'free ride' could have cost me my life had I gone.

I reached out to several friends as I packed myself up because I was stirring the pot of Universal energies and things were moving too fast for me to handle on my own. People who cared or could see I was losing touch with reality were worried and I was doing my best to keep up with the intense energies I felt coursing through me.

It wasn't until I called my Dad to tell him about all the magick I'd been experiencing that his wife, Bonnie, broke my trance and helped me see the metaphoric manhole I was about to fall into when she shouted from the background "Holy shit, she's going to get kidnapped!" and it was the first time that idea even entered my mind. Suddenly I saw clearly that it was the perfect set up and I changed my mind about going with him just in time.

The man showed up at my door soon after but instead of welcoming him in I used the latch to crack the door open and look into my expectant chariot driver's eyes where I sensed bad intentions and told him I would not go with him and he needed to leave. He stayed on the balcony outside my suite for a while calling our mutual acquaintance I suspect but I'd told the black magi he'd mistrusted the man and I wasn't going anywhere with the one he'd sent to get me. He had already departed from the hotel so was no longer present to change my mind but surprisingly my trust for him lasted longer; months later when I cut the energetic cords he reached out again immediately after because vampires feed energetically, not just physically.

While I have no proof this was the men's intended outcome what I do know is that I am grateful I trusted myself to listen when a message of warning came through my loved ones as messages generally do.

It's like the joke about the devout man in a flood zone who trusted God to save him; as he boarded his windows neighbours came by and offered him a ride but he said 'God will save me' so declined and kept on praying. As the waters started rising he moved to the second story of his home and saw a boat going by that stopped and offered him a ride but he declined believing God was going to save him. Shortly after the water levels had forced him onto the roof, a rescue helicopter flew overhead and threw down a ladder but he held firm that God was going to save him. He drowned and when he met his maker he asked why he didn't come to save him not seeing that spirit acts through the living.

Who knows what could have happened to me had I not heeded the guidance I feel I was sent but the reality is that human trafficking preys on weakness and vulnerability which is why learning to trust our intuition and the resonance of truth is more than just woo-woo spiritual stuff. It's a vital mode of self-defence that must be honed and is part of the SPECIAL Practice that PEACEFULL INNER Warriors United and Untied are called to intentionally foster.

Intuition, Following Hunches & Our Deepest FEAR

25

We become the average of the people we spend our time with and the books we read, was the saying of old. Now we must add the movies and shows we watch, the things we buy and the places we go as the available input our environment now offers is significantly greater than any other time in history; you better believe it's intentional too.

The busier we are the less opportunity we have to pause and integrate the sensory input in our midst and the corp-orations know it. We're taught autonomy (the right or condition of self-government in accordance with objective morality) and independence are the goal, and many believe doing 'whatever it takes' to secure this illusionary state is ok. But once again we must ask ourselves "what is the point of gaining the world while losing our soul in the process?"

Intuition is the guide our soul hired ahead of time, before the light in us was limited to the form of our body or the time space continuum of this Earthly REALITY we see to be Realistic Evidence Appearing Legit In Tomorrow's Yesterday. It's the tuition that was paid before we incarnated to help us make choices that will empower instead of destroy our cells and others. Like the infamous good angel and devil on our shoulder that influence our decision-making process and the resulting life we get to lead, our in-tuition is our guide; whether we direct our attention toward False Emotion Appearing Real or faith is our choice and will determine which side of the Divine we feed.

As creatures of comfort we often tend to hold ourselves hostage to the past and view our present as a reflection of our potential when the truth is that our pre-sent REALITY is a reflection of our previous level of awareness of our potential which directly impacts our magnetic field. Our future will reflect the choices we make now and recognizing how our (free) will works with spirit (awareness) to merge in the heart and bring forward our heart's desires (manifestation) helps us leverage the creative process to work for us instead of against us.

Drunvalo Melchizedek wrote a book about the toroidal field of the heart called *Living in the Heart: How to Enter Into the Sacred Space Within the Heart* which describes the centre point from which our life force stems. He says there is a point in the heart that surgeons know they cannot touch or it will be 'lights out' or 'game over' for the patient being operated on. It must be respected as the re-generator of our life force energy that is said to radiate up and around to create an apple-like effect energetically; our heart, mind, soul and body are like the apple seeds while the energy field around us can be likened to the flesh and meat of the apple itself. Our thoughts truly become things just as James Allen wrote in *As A Man Thinketh* which contains secrets of the Universe if you have eyes to see or ears to hear and willingness to apply the insights to your mind's eye which is where all things are first created.

Just as an apple seed contains a substance (amygdalin) that releases cyanide into the blood stream when chewed and digested in large amounts, we must begin to see that toxic thought seeds work within our energy field and creative process in the same way. For this reason we must begin to take better care of the real estate being fought for in this thought war for consciousness that we are response-able for as the rulers of our respective INNER kingdoms.

We must start to consider distractions as thieves of our TEEAM that we need no longer feed, just as the Cherokee grandfather told his grand-one about the wolves within him who were fighting one another. In the Sacred Sojourn of the Soul it's the 'Dark-Light of the Soul' phase of transformation when we must battle the BS within to overcome the cognitive dissonance we experience when we introduce a baby belief to a household that likes things just the way they are.

T. Harv Eker makes a great point that if you aim to be comfortable you will never be rich because you will always limit yourself to continue playing small whereas if you aim to be rich you will find yourself very comfortable with a life you are proud to live. Keep in mind that true wealth is not material in nature but reflects our ability to be content where we are with what we have or are doing. It is the difference between states of emotion and states of being pre-sent and the respective spirals of each.

Marianne Williamson's poem "Our Deepest Fear" is one of my favourites and was first introduced to me by an extended family member who inadvertently helped me on my way by giving me a copy of Harv's book *Secrets of the Millionaire Mind* which I ironically never finished but which opened the door for me to join my first Mastermind on Napoleon Hill's book *Think and Grow Rich*. To both Maria, and Deb who became the first Life Success Consultant I knew personally and hired to experience the process I intended to one day offer myself, I am forever grateful, as I am to Marianne (Williamson), T. Harv (Eker), Napoleon (Hill), Louise (Hay) and all the other influencers who guided me on my journey here.

It's a reminder that we may never know the impact we will have on another's life, for better or worse, but we cannot give with any attachment to how our gift is received; like the proverb about planting the oak tree we never expect to sit under the shade of we must shift our focus back to the moment we are in where all our power exists.

As John Maxwell says "we must be rivers (of blessings) instead of reservoirs" even if others are given credit for creating that which we originated, we must create anyway. Marianne's powerful poem is often attributed to Nelson Mandela but can be found in her book *A Return To Love* which I have yet to read fully but these words I have learned by heart:

> Our deepest fear is not that we are inadequate.
> Our deepest fear is that we are powerful beyond measure.

It is our light, not our darkness
That most frightens us.

We ask ourselves
Who am I to be brilliant, gorgeous, talented, fabulous?
Actually, who are you *not* to be?
You are a child of God.

Your playing small does not serve the world.
There's nothing enlightened about shrinking
So that other people won't feel insecure around you.

We are all meant to shine,
As children do.
We were born to make manifest
The glory of God that is within us.

It's not just in some of us;
It's in everyone.

And as we let our own light shine,
We unconsciously give other people permission to
do the same.
As we're liberated from our own fear,
Our presence automatically liberates others.

When we dare to share our heart song without fear of who will revere (or condemn) us for it we impact the world in a way only an artist (creative) can. And what the youth of our day need to remember is that creativity is not just child's play, it is the work of one who has claimed authority over their lives and dared to uplift and inspire others in the process.

And with that being said, from personal experience, I would encourage you to see how the virtual realities we have moved toward take us away from being present where we are with the ones we are there with.

In many ways, as I've already shared, I feel like I lived a pre-COVID lifestyle when I returned from England and started rebuilding my life from my brother's childhood bedroom where I landed as a sales rep for the JMT. I painted his room gold with pricey paint that gave me the effect I desired given how much time I knew I'd be spending in there when I took on a home-based role. I'd asked myself what colour would inspire me and gold was the answer so I sought that which matched my intuitive hunch and I still have part of the can left which I've used to paint 'accent pieces' ever since; it was a great investment regardless of whether others thought so or not.

While transplanting some baby marigold plants I started from last year's seeds this morning I was listening to an audio of Florence Scovel Shinn's book *The Magic Path of Intuition* and am reminded that the way I've lived my life is uncommon because of how often I have followed my intuition. It feels a significant element to bring in now for your re-mind-(h)er to follow your inner guidance system, remembering that people will forget what you said, they may even forget what you did, but they'll never forget the way you made them feel. And believe you-me I've got some relationships to heal and deal with so if it's with you, I send love and am doing my best to do better! "I'm sorry, please forgive me, thank you, I love you" (Ho'oponopono prayer)!

One of the most poignant examples of following my intuition took place near the beginning of my life in England for a relationship that came with great benefits and major energetic liabilities too. Were it not for this early act of inspired guidance I would not have likely stayed for the 3.5 years I did given the lack of respect my then partner and provider had for me but I am grateful because I learned and grew a lot from it, particularly because of the people I met, the trainings I took and the friends some became.

In the first month I was there my ex and I went to get vegetables at a Farmer's Market on the other side of Worcester to where we lived in an old renovated hydroelectric mill on the outskirts of town. You'd know it by the towering chimney and beautiful loft apartments that have replaced its original function.

I'd got him to drop me off in town on our way back so I could look around and acquaint myself with my new surroundings as he had work to do and I was trying to figure out what to do now that I lived in a new country where I only knew him, his kids and his ex-wife who was kind considering how uncomfortable the situation would have been for her; their divorce had only come through the night before I flew to move out there and the split was because he'd got into personal growth and felt he outgrew their marriage. She was devastated and he was focused on himself and what he wanted despite the toll it took on their family. I, on the other hand, was 18 years younger than him without children or lived experience to see how selfish he was plus I needed to fit into his life if I wanted the life I'd given up mine in Canada to pursue. My inner prostitute was living in her scared side then and I was willing to pay the price until I wasn't; the end of 'us' was when the sacred side of this archetype was activated in me and I got to feel the difference in power that comes with that kind of internal shift.

But truly the major reason I was able to stay in that relationship without losing myself in the process for as long as I did was because of this day early on. I followed my intuition to go into a charity shop downtown to see if they had another book by Marianne Williamson. I'd found a copy of one of her books over the weekend when we'd walked downtown and perused a different charity shop. We hadn't had time to visit this one so when he dropped me off after the market that day I'd went in to see why this shop called to me.

Nothing stood out so I asked a shop attendant where I might find another book by Marianne, which I didn't even really want but felt called to ask about. They suggested I go to another charity shop in Reindeer Court which meant nothing to me so I asked for directions. They said to go down the alleyway opposite the shop we were in and take my first right to the end, then take my first left and it would be right in front of me, except my coach training helped me notice something many may have overlooked.

When the woman said go right her head motioned to the left and when she said go left her head motioned to the right and because of my training I knew our body language often tells the truth more than our words so I decided to follow her words knowing I could always go back and track where her body language said the place would be.

Her words led me straight to a crystal shop which having just moved there without much money I didn't really want to buy anything but trusted there was a reason for being led astray.

I started looking at the inventory quietly while another customer asked the woman working there about a crystal and her answer was deep and profoundly insightful; I commented on this and the door of conversation was opened. An hour later I left the shop with her number and made my first friend outside of the relationship the rest of my life there was based on. Another woman named Maria became an ally and mentor I valued more than words can express who helped me see the covert manipulation I was subject to in a relationship that had little tolerance for any inconvenient emotionality.

Were it not for Maria I would have likely left England months after moving there when my inherited ex-wife sent me a text to say "Happy anniversary, would have been 10 years today. Forgot to mention it when I dropped the kids off." I was understandably triggered by this Freudian slip and while my 23 year old self tried to figure out how I felt about receiving this message, he defensively told me she'd obviously accidentally texted me instead of him (which didn't feel much better to me) and he wasn't going to have his children around my energy while I was emotionally distressed and charged as I was. So he took the kids to a playcentre and told me that if I hadn't sorted myself out by the time they got back I could get on the next flight to 'Canadiania' as he called it. I internalized his projections and did sort myself out by the time they got back but hadn't recognized the emotionally abusive tactics I'd just experienced until confiding in my new friend over coffee shortly after; that was not a scene I wanted to share with those at home to concern them so without her I would have taken his projections on and worn them with shame like he'd (unconsciously) intended me to.

Over the years there were several of those kinds of suppressive and manipulative exchanges that Maria helped me unpack without feeling like I was crazy and so it was that I learned how to tell when something is mine (emotionally) versus when I am told it's mine but really it's someone else's projection they want me to wear for their own reasons. This served me invaluably during my imprisonment in 2019 so to all involved I am grateful and to those in relationship dynamics triggered by this I feel for you and you deserve better. People treat us the way we teach them is acceptable so own your part so you can strengthen yourself but don't take on projections that aren't yours lest they weigh you down and attract more of the same.

Following my intuition that day in 2012 changed the trajectory of my life because 'Star Priestess' Maria Jones is an old soul with ancient wisdom she shared generously with me that would have been nearly impossible to find on my own; I didn't know what I was looking for, I just knew when things felt resonant and nourishing to my soul and every time we got together I felt better for having spent time with her. She opened my eyes to the sacred nature of crystals and their energetic properties, explained the influence of my natal birth chart in relation to the times we were in, and introduced me to many hidden gems in friends she had collected like a bouquet that cannot be purchased.

Zorah Cholmondeley was one of these beautiful souls whose passion for nature, Shamanism and healing through plants, crystals, elemental beings and emotional release practices helped me tremendously during my time in England and beyond. Her book *The Enchanted Garden* can introduce you to Zorah's sacred approach to life and the mysteries of it which greatly expanded my awareness of the unseen. Were it not for Maria I may not have met Zorah and both women significantly impacted my life not just because of the sacred information they shared with me but also because of the space they held for me as I organically unfolded in the safety of compassionate and caring community connections.

Were it not for following my hunch to ask about a book I felt called to look for, I wouldn't have discovered the (then) unpublished teachers that hunch guided me to. I share this to remind you that the sacred sojourn of the soul is not a path any book or guru can guide you to or through because each will only hold a key to unlock the next unseen door that will grant you entry to the next test, trial or tribulation that helps you call forth inner resilience that facing that experience will help you to strengthen. Trust the process and your own organic unfoldment more than the standard guidance others will offer based on what they think would be best for you; you will be the one that lives with the consequences of your choices so dare to take the unchartered path you came here to blaze with your life.

Turning inward and learning to trust the guru within will help you to create the life you came here to live that others won't believe is possible until you make it happen. Trust yourself to feel your way through life, one day at a time, and celebrate yourself each time you follow an intuitive hunch (one that resonates with your heart rather than your head) that opens a door you may not have even known you were looking for.

Our Furry Companions, Choosing Life After Death & The Right Use Of Will

26

Weeks before I started this version of the book my beloved Julius Romeo got attacked and I knew our time together was limited. He had underlying health issues and was showing signs of his 'geriatric status' but had been happy and healthy despite the fact I hadn't taken him to a vet since before my hospitalized imprisonment experience in 2019 when I tuned into the business of sickness and the in-doctor-nation (indoctrination) process being culturally propagated. I believe the current vaccination schedule of pets and people alike is directly correlated to the present endemic of disease in both that reflects the complicated webs we weave when we leave parts of ourselves behind as the current programming would have us do.

> *Endemic: a disease or condition regularly found among particular people or in a certain area.*
> *Epidemic: Epi is Greek for 'upon or above' and demos for 'people'*
> *Pandemic: Pan is Greek for 'all' and demos for 'people'*

I mention this here because my beloved cat brought me back to re-member the sacred nature of life in our final days together before his euthanasia which I approved for reasons I believed to ultimately be best for him. It was a similar but very different situation to the one I'd been put in two years before that led to a mental breakdown that got me reconnected to real life and reintegrated into the community where I live right before the Certificate Of Vex ID-AI Pendemic began when the isolated lifestyle I'd had up till then became part of the 'new normal'. It was yet another gift in disguise even though I couldn't see it at the time.

The night Julius was attacked was a Wednesday. I was distracted when I let him out the window at suppertime failing to remember I'd seen a stray tom cat around the house earlier. I was feeling overwhelmed by all the energy I was putting out without return for all the investments I was making, personally and professionally, and I was soothing my unrest by smoking weed in excess. My friend, Star Priestess Maria Jones, had warned me to quit before my 'Saturn Return' in 2015 when the cosmic life coach (Saturn) returned to the same place in my natal chart to highlight patterns I needed to clear lest I got stuck with their consequences and I'd failed to heed her warning; it takes place between ages 27–31, 56–60 and 84–90 so beware where you are so you can heed the lessons yours comes to teach you. The seven years of hell she'd forecast if I didn't stop unfolded as predicted and bring us to how Julius' death helped me finally commit to upgrading the WEB of my cell-F image to weed marijuana out and stop leaking energy through self-doubt.

I'd observed him closely when he came inside that night, slower than usual and walking tenderly which was when I remembered the bully cat I'd seen around earlier. I checked him over and found some surface scratches on his leg and ears but certain movements led me to suspect he'd sustained internal damage. While his purr returned the next day and he was still mobile, his litter box remained empty despite his efforts to relieve himself and Saturday morning I called the vets for help. The last thing I wanted was for them to try to 'catch him up' with all the shots he'd missed in the years since his last visit but they assured me that would not be the case.

They closed early Saturday and only had an opening in the time it would take for me to shuttle him to their office so I accepted the appointment, grabbed the dusty cat carrier from the garage and coerced him in; he hated car rides and normally meowed the whole ride in but this time he was largely quiet; he needed help and trusted me after fourteen years of loving him to the best of my ability so together we rode quietly to his doom.

When we arrived I had to call reception for a phone consult before the vet came out to collect him for inspection. I cried when I found out I couldn't go in there with him and not too long after the woman acting as a vet came out with the bad news. His bladder was the size of a grapefruit and needed to be drained but the catheter installment required anesthesia and his age and heart issues meant his chances weren't good, plus because they were closing early he'd have to be sent elsewhere to do it. My other choice was to be with him while they put him down in the office before closing time which I knew was his better option given the chunky energy I'd noticed for a while and suspected was some form of cancer which the vet also alluded to. His quality of life was limited and I just wanted to be with him.

I dawned a mask to go in which is a rarity and I sat with him for as long as I could while conscious of the fact that the longer we waited the more uncomfortable he got. I cried while he purred and soaked up the love I gave him, before they took him out to get the injection spot ready and then brought him back in to get the job done. I sat on the floor eye level to him and within seconds of the solution being injected into the port his head fell to the couch, he made a squeak I can only relate to the sound of his soul being freed from the genie bottle of his body, and shortly after his lungs made their final move. He was gone but his body remained. I paid the bill, put him in the cardboard coffin they gave me with the lid open and I took his body home to let Papa say goodbye before I buried him in the woods where several other family pets had been laid to rest over the years my Grandparents have owned the farm I grew up on.

I'd rolled two joints that morning with the remaining bud a friend had given me and had smoked part of one before calling the vet. After I got back I contemplated smoking the rest of it before burying him but it felt dishonouring, especially because I'll always remember the look he gave me when I was trying to offer him healing the day before, after smoking, and he looked into my eyes as if to say "O, you humans." For cats are zen masters who have mastered presence without need for complication or complexity and unconditionally love the one(s) they choose as he had me fourteen years before when he fell asleep in my arms the first time I held him, as if he'd found his home and could finally rest. And in closing the chapter of life with him I decided to bury the part of me that was willing to weaken myself as weed does our auric field which is, I believe, why it was legalized in Canada when it was.

I kept those dubies in my desk drawer until my pre-trial hearing on May 4, nearly a month later, and then gave them to my law man who had encouraged me to face the music of my emotions lest I have to face my denials in the form of persecutors trained in the art of war. We walked to the woods together to discard them after my showdown with a man and woman acting on behalf of a corrupted corps(e) that pays them money backed by nothing but the people's trust, for doing the "devil's dirty work" when it is them who will pay the ultimate price for their choice to cause harm to one who knows who and whose I am.

And so it is that I've cleaned up my act, auric field, body, mind and soul in the month and a half since my beloved companion departed from this world to be whole with the source of it all until he returns in another form, should that be his will and wish.

I share this story because that cat loved me even when I wasn't loving myself fully.

My law man recommended Ceanne DeRohan's *Right Use of Will* series early on in our tutelage which I read my way through, often with Julius at my side, in the months leading up to this turning point in my life. The blue book is the first, given the eight make up the colours of the rainbow (and chakras), and is subtitled "Healing and Evolving the Emotional Body" which is what we're collectively being called to do now.

To ensure I spelt Ceanne's name correctly I grabbed the blue book and flipped to a page to see what 'book medicine' called me in that moment which you can do with any book that calls to you too; instead of starting at the beginning and reading through to the end, consider flipping to a page and reading the passage your eyes are drawn to. You can do this with movies or YouTube videos too because sometimes the whole thing is more than you need in the moment; follow your inner guidance to what you feel called to and your 'medicine' will be there for you if you're willing to consider it.

Here's the passage on page 31 that called to me and feels relevant to us all at this time:

> "An understanding you need about protecting yourself when you are surrounded by a reality that does not seem to agree with your own personal choices is this: Get in touch with why you are there, process everything you can find in yourself regarding this, in the way that I am explaining here, and see what happens. I am going to help you with this, because I can see that the reality on Earth is pressuring for widespread conformity. You also need to do your part by developing and using your discernment. By taking responsibility for yourself, you can clear up everything that holds you to a reality, or part of a reality, that you do not like. Because misunderstandings have been in place for so long, this can seem to be a tall order; much more complex than many people have thought when they began, but if you do not begin, you cannot get there. When you no longer have anything within you that attracts what you do not want, your right place will feel good to you because it will not have anything that you do not like."

Smoking weed, or any other coping mechanism that suppresses, represses, depresses, or compresses energies in motion (emotion) that need acceptance in order to be turned around keep us from being fully pre-sent where we are when we're there. And even though we may well have cannabinoid receptors that suggest marijuana is natural to us, we need to look at the bigger picture and the spiritual warfare current-lie at play on plan-ET Earth (heart shifted) that requires reordering NOW.

The New World Order (NWO) is the corrupted version of the Newly Ordered World (NOW) that has been running the show since the beginning of his-story. The Fabian Society, Vatican, British Monarchy, Free Masons and many more secret societies are in on this sick plot for world domination and full control of life within it, but the higher you go the more you get to know so most don't see the evil plan until they've invested so much TEEAM into their membership they don't feel they can turn around and survive the shadow they have to walk through as they return to who and whose they were before they thought they needed more.

Now it is time for us to shift into writing our story instead of his which requires we stop taking the pre-scripts an outer authority and author-i-tie my identity to would tell us is good for us when we're the ones who must live with the consequences of taking bad add-vice. And what the 'powers that be' don't tell the ones indoctrinated into the corrupted system designed to Save You Significant Time Energy Money and more is that those who act on behalf of a corps to harm another take on the karmic consequences for doing so; ignorance is not bliss, it just means you will bring your entanglements with you into your next incarnation without context for why certain patterns seem to follow you.

What if we came here so we can create heaven on Earth and enjoy the one life we get to live as the organic original we can only be if we protect and defend the sacred lands of the kingdom within?

What if we have a chance now to do the impossible by choosing to call our power back to the pre-sent moment where we can truly be there for one another without doing so for the sake of what we can get from the one we pretend to love?

What if we dared to do the INNER work to heal ourselves and our cells so that we no longer cause harm to one another or the heart of Ma Terre that we all share?

It's time to realize we are at the turning point in our story and our souls are the ones that will pay the ultimate price for the choices we make while we are here because death is not the end of life. It's just the end of life as we knew it.

We live in a Uni-verse with a Great Orchestra Director that needs every single one of us to play our part to the best of our ability by remembering that we win the lottery every day we wake up and get to live another day. Money and material success are not the prize, time is, and we win 86,400 seconds to do with as we please each day. So in the end we will have to account for how we invested our winnings before we get to play again as a new character in the game of life we are all playing, until we're not.

Re-legions and his-story write about the 'great ones' who lived and what they did because their lives impacted the world, for better or worse, and we've been trained to re-member them so that we fail to see that our lives are the greatest story that has not yet been written because we're writing it as we live it.

All the spirits and entities being channeled, by us who are alive to receive the messages, have no power without us and so it is time for us to stop being used by corpses who are power-less without us because the truth is that we are power-full and must re-member our power exists in the pre-sent NOW moment where all choices are made.

The Power Of Our Choices, INNER WEBs & Codes To Live By
27

As we near the end of the book that rewrote me before this version of me was birthed through my lived experience, I want to discuss the WEB of our INNER Kingdom and how pre-sent influences have been doing their best to keep the scared side of our nature in charge and running the show (of our lives).

"If you don't respect me, you don't get (to have access to) me" is the hard line I finally drew in the sand of my own metaphoric lands in the energy den (E-den) I am a guard in that helped me finally become a book Mama as I'd tried becoming for years before my WEB allowed me to finally do it. Consider what kind of guard in the E-den of you you're being.

Words are a way we measure worth which is why they are the sacred swords that either set us free or keep us in captivity.

In the year it's taken for me to address the implied charge against my person for violating an Act I never agreed to play in when the con was sent for my consciousness I have learned a lot about life and the power of our choices.

Back in 2017 I actually flew to Sedona to attend a workshop on "The Power of Our Choices" with Caroline Myss whose work I was introduced to in 2013 when I became a Soul Realignment Practitioner and read her assigned text "*The Anatomy of the Spirit: The Seven Stages of Power and Healing.*" I have read many of Caroline's books and went to Sedona with the intention of getting a picture with her because at that time I placed a lot of weight on my online identity and a picture with a woman I often reference was great blogging material.

I was living on my own in Paris (with Julius) at the time and while a Christmas special offer had given me an influx of commissions I was grateful for, internal changes within the company had me on the chopping block at the time I booked this conference but Goom had encouraged me to go despite the uncertainty of my situation. My Grandma Donna (I called her Goom) was one of my best friends in the whole world and I know for sure I wouldn't be the woman I am today without her influence; she supported me and my alternative outlook on life as much as she could even though she didn't fully understand it. She was one of my greatest teachers, both in life and death, and I am beyond grateful I came into this world through her son whose birthday (May 30) is the day I submitted this manuscript to be published – I love you Dad!

With Goom's blessings, I committed to the trip and saw a rideshare request by another participant on the event's Facebook page who was renting a vehicle at the airport and staying an extra day to do the Pink Jeep Tours of Sedona's red rocks which sounded fun. We agreed to split the cost of the rental to Enchantment Resort where the workshop was hosted and share the adventure after together too. She'd wrote a book about her own archetypes based on all of Caroline's workshops she'd flown around the country to attend so was *very* attached to knowing her guru best; she helped ingrain the pronunciation of Myss as 'mis' which really pissed me off, the way she did it, but I was facing many of my own shadow aspects in that dynamic too. Energetically it was a lot of work for me and I let an unspoken feeling of obligation to 'stick together' keep me in the front row, in the same seat, for most of the event; usually I move around and sit where I feel called at conferences but guilt and a great seat kept me bound to an energy I felt drained by, even though she was a lovely woman.

I broke away to do my own thing during breaks but felt an underlying neediness I fed unconsciously as we do when dealing with dysfunctional energies and the entities that come with them;

I limited myself because my suppressed irritation lowered my vibe and let her projections become part of my REALITY. On the drive I'd shared how much Caroline's work had impacted me and how excited I was to get a picture with her that I could add to my collection of 'famous people' I'd met in my travels. She'd dashed my hopes early on by referencing a past I wasn't present for as proof positive Caroline doesn't do pictures at her events. That may be true for others but it only became true for me because I let this woman's BS into my creative process and thus co-created that experience.

Back then I leaked energy carelessly because I didn't realize how dangerous doing so is to the creative process. Thoughts lose their power when shared without support which is why confession helps many people surrender their burdens and move forward without the same level of shame carried before the energy is broken up by the spoken word; the same happens when we share our intentions so be full of care with who you share.

It was a profound lesson that jarred my ego for quite a while after though I'm glad I got over myself to still attend a private event Caroline spoke at in Toronto the next year anyway; one powerful idea applied can change the trajectory of our lives and we never know where it will come from or who by. Getting in the room with people who stretch our mind and sense of possibility increases the value of our virtues (habits of mind, heart, and behavior), contributing to an enhanced sense of self-worth if we're willing to face the shadows as they show up.

We must see how the letter W is made of two Vs (Value & Virtues) put together to reflect the fact wars are won one battle at a time and so is life. Furthermore, what if life need no longer be the war zone internal division has led us to believe is 'just the way it is' because it's always been that way?

What if shifting out of that BS required we change the habits of our own mind, heart and behavior to be the change we seek in this world by shifting the patterns within us first?

What if we dared to believe in our own significance as co-creators incarnate?

Like microcosms of the macrocosmic experience that life is, clearing up garbage within our cells and self-image leads to a cleaner reality because we are all but mirrors reflecting one another back to the one we judge when they are simply a mirror to reveal what we have yet to heal within ourselves.

We have been told we need to be more, do more and have more to be enough and after living with that story for years and unpacking that illusion from my own identity I have come to see how we can take it from its scared side of not enough to its sacred side of standing in our power, to-gather, to say "we've had enough" of the lies.

We've all heard the allegedly misattributed quote "The only thing necessary for the triumph of evil is for good men to do nothing" because we lose the will to try and oomph (enthusiasm, or energy) to do our best when victory is not assured. But what in this world is ever truly guaranteed except death and taxes we're told, except did you know the Income Tax Act expired with the War Measures Act so that's technically not true either?

FEAR makes us believe safety and survival are the most important aspects of life but that is only because keeping us distracted by lower level needs means we don't have energy left to aspire to greater things; this cultural emphasis is intentional because the more internal tension that can be created within each man, woman and child, the easier we are to con and troll.

Troll: to harass, criticize, or antagonize (someone) especially by provocatively disparaging or mocking public statements, postings, or acts

Con: something (such as a ruse) used deceptively to gain another's confidence

We have to stop throwing each other away and keeping our sphere of influence small and closed off because that is how wars rage on and the poem "First They Came" becomes reality for those who never thought the war would come their way. We'll feel scared of others if we're scared of so many aspects of ourselves that we stop trusting ourselves to do the right thing when we're called to do it. And because we are insecure we project that energy onto others and look for the worst instead of the best.

We limit ourselves and our possibilities because we buy into the lack, limitation and scarcity mentality that we tie our identity to when the truth is that our outer REALITY reflects the world within. While insecurity makes us feel unsafe and insignificant, INNER security helps us feel at home wherever we are because we have a portable sense of home or 'safe zone' we bring with us. And we trust ourselves enough to listen to the voice of in-tuition that lets us know danger or evil is in our midst when we feel it.

Esteem is an opinion or judgement about someone or something's worth or value that determines the regard in which one is held.

We respect what we esteem and we dis(respect) that which we believe to be less than.

What is truly ours cannot be walled off from us unless we put up walls within our own heart which is the creative source of our REALITY and which reflects the BS writing the script of life as the one and only us there ever has or will be. Daring to do the INNER work means dropping the walls (of words) that previously kept us feeling safely separate from that which we FEAR and helps us find the silver lining of whatever situations we find ourselves in.

Self-esteem is directly tied to our beliefs about ourselves, the world and the people in it and even though the current cult(ure) has savagely promoted sacrifice of self and others for the sake of profits and personal gain, it's time for us to shift our focus onto legacy and contribution as the cause backing our actions. I believe this is how we move ourselves back to the creative (be-cause) end of the cause and effect equation. This is how we shift from being REACTIVE to CREATIVE and respect ourselves more for contributing to the world in the way only we can.

Here's the secret the elite never wanted us to re-member: contribution isn't just about the big stuff in life, it's about the thousands of choices we make every day and how those effect the way we play at life and the people we're in it with.

A quote by Ralph Waldo Emerson says "To find the best in others; to give (of) one's self; to leave the world a bit better, whether by a healthy child, a garden patch or a redeemed social condition; to have played and laughed with enthusiasm and sung with exaltation; to know even one life has breathed easier because you have lived – this is to have succeeded."

Don Miguel Ruiz wrote a short but significant book called *The Four Agreements: A Toltec Wisdom Guide* which reveals a power-full honour code to transform your life and enhance your self-esteem in the process. These four agreements are:

1. Be impeccable with your word
2. Don't take anything personally
3. Don't make assumptions
4. Always do your best

Dare I say these are foundational principles to keep in mind as you design the life you lead as you be-come someone you respect because you trust yourself to act with honour.

Doing so will absolutely strengthen your WEB of self-worth, self-esteem and self-belief in a way that allows you to aim higher by allowing your desires to rise to the surface like the cream of the crop we previously thought we were not.

If not you then who will do what you uniquely came to this world equipped for?

What if your whole reason for being born was to be on someone's path on the day they planned to be their last and because you smiled at them when they thought no one cared whether they lived or died they changed their mind and chose life? What if everything else in your entire life was a bonus because you accomplished this trajectory changing task you had no idea meant everything to that soul in that moment? What if it were really that simple?

You may not have worldly status, title, position or prestige (yet) but when you choose to lead your own life responsibly you offer a vibrational example to those who see you as someone who cares and they raise their own standard because of your example. That is why we are here together, to gather in common unity and walk each other home to our own respective heart centres.

For years I've got to meet and interact with people in 'high places' due to my willingness to get in rooms, trainings and gatherings I felt called to attend. I have also acted on inspiration to meet souls in 'low (emotional) places' who have touched my life in the way no professional ever has. My travel buddy in Sedona taught me as much as Caroline did that trip because the contrast offered me clarity I wouldn't have went out of my way to learn intentionally. Energetic boundaries were a common theme between all of these interactions that have helped me gain clarity as to what's mine, what's being projected onto me, and what I've picked up that has served its purpose and is ready to be shifted.

Growing up the adults in my life always seemed to have answers to my questions and I thought that meant they were smarter than me because I wasn't so sure about things. I questioned things and noticed gaps I was insecure about while other people seemed to know and trust 'the facts' in a way I didn't. My natural Passion, Enthusiasm, Authenticity and Encouraging attitude was missing Clarity for a long time because I compared myself to the false front of confidence so many wear without facing the underlying emotions I've been moving through every step of the way. Vulnerability and transparency have always been so important to me that I presumed others were just better at dealing with their insecurities than me; it hadn't occurred to me that most weren't digging for the roots of the BS running their lives in the same committed way I was.

When I met Seth Godin at the International Maxwell Certification event I got to be Paul Martinelli's assistant at in 2017 he gave me a signed copy of his book which I've kept in view for the last year as the cover has a picture of a younge woman with piercing eyes and a title that reads: *WHAT TO DO WHEN IT'S YOUR TURN (and it's always your turn)*. Indeed it is!

Instead of looking down the line of competitors at the start of a race to see who our competition is, we must call on our highest self to help us to do our absolute best without holding back due to insecurity any longer than we already have.

Holding back contracts our expansion and jeopardizes our sense of INNER security by creating cells of FEAR that threaten our Passion, Enthusiasm, Authenticity, Clarity and Encouragement in future NOW moments when we are next called to put our best foot forward. Let's dare to do the INNER work of facing ourselves to get fully committed to showing up fully, without being distracted or displaced within ourselves so that we can be all we're meant to be.

From there, the WEB we weave will be full of beauty, just as are we.

SIN, Standing In Our Power & Settling No More

It's been challenging to figure out how to write this final chapter of the book that took five years for me to finally write in a month which was my original goal (less the five years) but I'm over the story of not enough and 'too much' and all the woulda, coulda, shoulda beens in between. While this chapter marks the end of one season of my life, it also marks the start of another where respect and self-actualization are accepted as guiding principles that bring about a more functional experience of community life that values people and truth over profits and lie-ability. It seemed impossible to those I told during my awakening but it's part of my mission in this life and I don't need permission to be fully committed to doing my part by starting with the one life I get to lead as me.

The metaphoric chapter of lies without liability we are now called to close will not surrender without a fight so long as men and women volunteer to take up arms and harm one another for a control program that has become obsolete. It is also the ones using their pens to sign away the rights of men that must consider the commonality of hues of our skin and the Ma Terre we share instead of the LAW they've been working for in sin.

Don Miguel Ruiz says "A sin is anything that you do which goes against yourself. Everything you feel or believe or say that goes against yourself is a sin." Now let that sink in as we bring about the Newly Ordered World the New Orderly World can be if we call for it to be NOW.

A truth-full reality is possible and will not come about without its challenges but we have enjoyed the lifestyles we've got to lead until now because of those who stood for us and now it's our turn to return the favour for those who come after us. Robin Sharma famously said "Change is hardest at the beginning, messiest in the middle and best at the end" and we must believe in ourselves to be the change we seek if we are to leave a legacy worth inheriting for those who come through us but do not belong to us. This requires we know how to stand in the truth of who and whose we are because we fought for our own rights to be our true and authentic selves fully and are able to pass on the fruits of our labour.

We must do as we say and remain standing in honour even when telling the truth costs us the life we had when our soul was bought and paid for by the devil who lived backwards and corrupted the whole cart of apples that reflect our heart's magnetic power.

Hardened hearts have hidden walls that breed insecurity because we don't feel safe as we are and believe we must earn our way in a world that doesn't feel safe to play the game of life the way we wish to; the buck must stop with us for the fiat currency we current-lie use to trade our lives for is backed by nothing but the faith we put into the ones who make rules to use our energy for profits over people. No longer is that an accept-able way forward and when the old world falls we must be there for one another without offering add-vice when space to organically unfold is how we truly come back into wholeness and work together to truly build back better.

It starts by taking the suits off the men and women who are 'in the know' so the corporate umbrella of protection no longer holds back the karmic consequences of the fact they have intentionally sold out their fellow man, woman and child for the sake of profits backed by nothing but our trust.

Fiat: an authoritative or arbitrary order, determination, decree or dictate

Fiat money: legal-tender (paper money or coins) that have face values far exceeding their commodity values and are not redeemable in gold or silver.

Essentially what that means is that the current currencies are backed by nothing but the faith and trust we've given to the corrupted hands hired to care for the public's interest. Which is where the lie falls flat.

We are living in a mixed war between the public and the private during an attempted corporatocratic takeover that requires men and women to act against our better judgement to go along with an evil agenda that limits free will and destroys the inheritance of future generations.

Corporatocracy: refers to an economic, political and judicial system controlled by corporations or corporate interests.

Here's what the corpse doesn't tell those signing or acting on its behalf: the man or woman with a conscience to choose is fully liable for all harm caused by the script they approve.

Menticide was meant to dumb down the general public and make sure we forgot who and whose we are and indoctrination programs taught us what to think instead of how to do it. The planning was intense and orchestrated like a well-oiled machine we've been cogs in, focused on our role without seeing the whole picture and how deadly the machine's intentions are.

We were fed lies from the time we emerged from the womb of mothers who'd been traumatized and contracted into a disempowered state too. Those who noticed the evil were locked up or taken out of circulation so as to not infect others with the unrest a zest for life brings up in the hearts of creative beings like we are. Except some of us woke up and faced our fears so they could not be used against us because we have nothing to hide we aren't willing to own up to. We will no longer carry the cross meant to hang us up to dry out on like I experienced when I tried to say my purpose was far greater than my status suggested; others doubted me because they had yet to see the vision that was in me to bring forward. This is just one piece of the puzzle that will make up the legacy I leave behind me as one fully committed to being the best I can be without needing anyone to be less for my choosing to stand in my power.

I remember hearing Oprah Winfrey say that her best friend Gayle King never stood in her shadow because she stood by Oprah's side in her own light without fright that others cared more for her companion. Some will, some won't, who cares.

We have been taught connecting the dots was about details and information but that was part of the fraud to keep us searching outside our cells for that which can only be found within, like the INNER power both Oprah and Gayle used to stand stronger together. Napoleon Hill described this as the Mastermind principle which is "the coordination of knowledge and effort between two or more people who work towards a definite purpose in a spirit of harmony...no two minds ever come together without thereby creating a third, invisible intangible force, which may be likened to a third mind."

This is the power of collective consciousness and we are at a tipping point where our greatest contribution to the world will be in finding harmony within ourselves and our cells; this embodiment of PEACE changes the energetic signature we show up with in our presence and it changes the vibe of those we come into contact with in the process. This is why connecting the dots is about calling the people back into community where we re-member the sacred nature of the NOW and stand together on common ground without need for statuses, titles or positions that tell us who has the power.

We each came here to preach the go-spell of the script-u-(a)re writing with the life you are living regardless of whether anyone celebrates you for it or not. Be like the oyster who transforms a grain of sand into a pearl simply because you can transmute your pain-full experiences into gains others can benefit from if they have the privilege of finding you or your words because you dared to do something different and created something the world would have went without if you hadn't.

We are the living souls incarnate here to live a life worthy of telling a story about and while the storyteller always has creative liberties with the details, our task is to care for one another and bring down the walls (of Jericho) within our own hearts so that we stop leaving one another out in the cold, alone, when we are meant to be all one in a better reality where no one gets left behind.

For far too long the status quo has kept the lid on our self-image low to the point where many limbo and tip toe through lives they let others decide on for them based on illusory limits.

> Quo: something received or given for something else
> Status: position or rank in relation to others

For far too long we have let the 'status quo' keep us down in the trenches trying to get by while the divide between the haves and 'have nots' grows and becomes ever more consuming. That is purposeful and only we can stop it from taking us all down with it. We can, we will, and we must trust our cells and one another to do it now despite the growing pains that come with maturing.

Power corrupts and absolute power corrupts absolutely, but empowerment is the process of becoming stronger and more confident, especially in controlling one's life and claiming one's rights which each of us must do as a man or woman, not some 'other' creation that is owned by the creator of the term as described in the Hierarchy of Creation.

Space is the creator of all's territory which is why the legal system only has jurisdiction over form, not substance, and requires 'color of law' to segregate and re-legion us into groups that can be pit against one another to ensure we babble on instead of build a better world to gather (together) in common unity (community).

When previous civilizations fell the legal professionals were the first to be hung for betraying the people and the people then paid the karmic consequences for choosing violence, just as the man and women acting as soldiers and officers in the line of duty do when they take a life or harm another too.

The 'frontlines' have moved even closer to home and it's time for us to own our scared side so we can return the sacred to the throne room of the kingdom within; it is time to drop the instruments of war so many arms have held so that our hands are clean and free to write a script we can love living and leaving in trust to those we must protect it for.

We came to this plan-ET to reconnect with the heart of Ma Terre and the sacred nature of life. Knowledge is the ledge we know because we learned the edge from someone else; wisdom is the result of lived experience we trust because we dared to apply our why to the way we live and walk our talk as we're meant to do.

What is the point of gaining the world if we lose our soul in the process?

What if instead the point of life was to become more whole in soul, body, mind and spirit instead and to do so we must let the dead bury the dead by mining our experiences for the lessons they gifted us with, instead of focusing on the wounds they left us with?

Corp-orations lack heart, soul, body and mind for they rely on ours and can't afford for us to take back our power as we must. We can, we will, and we are NOW because of your willingness to stop being bored and to go create something we enjoy instead.

That is the fun of life and the reward will be in the review we get to see of all the ways we made this world better for our having been here as the one and only us there ever has or will be. So go write the greatest story the world has ever seen with the life you get to lead as the conscious co-creator of the Great Orchestra Director you truly are and came here to be.

Epilogue

May 30 has always been a significant day for me because I've chose to place significant emotional events on this day as a way to play with and honour the man whose seed contributed to my creation. I got all three of my tattoos on this day, five years apart from each other, and also booked a speaking gig with our namesake city that I pulled out of and devastated myself because of in 2019.

Events are not what change us but everything that goes into the lead up to them and aftermath of them, and sometimes the noteworthy moments at them too.

In 2006 I got branded with INTEGRITY in a spot you can generally only see when I'm in a bikini or unclothed but hold no shame about because the body is not an object to be lusted after in my opinion, for it is the container of the GOD spark within we worship life in.

In 2011 I got the Chinese character for 'to attentively listen' stamped on my wrist in purple to reflect royalty as I believe we must see ourselves to be if we are to lead ourselves honorably by calling the kind king and quality queen to the throne within as one of the three earlier manuscripts described but didn't make it into this one. Every piece of the character I wear in plain view holds meaning for it is comprised of the ears, eyes, open heart, undivided attention to give respect to the speaker and the higher-self connection to the Divine that allows us to be fully present with the one we're attentively listening to.

In 2016 I got the hummingbird logo that became my brand on my foot so I could enjoy the art while in yoga and other places too. I had love wrote where my website sits in my logo and call it my "free-love tattoo" because I was going to write free but didn't want the monetary associations attributed to me; funny how I now see that being free owned me or its negative connotations wouldn't have held such a charge for me.

215

And now in 2022 I add "submitted first book's manuscript for publishing" to my reasons to celebrate the day my Dad blessed this Earth with his presence and paved the way for me.

He bought me my first rose quartz crystal and introduced me to a spiritual guide who has played a significant role in my life countless times; to both I am grateful.

He took me to get my bellybutton pierced when I was 13 because for two years I begged and drove a needle through it myself to prove my point when I was 11. My Mom still resents it and I no longer wear it, but have the hole from years wearing a ring I enjoyed while I did.

He took me to the Doctor's appointment and specialist appointment to get my sweat glands removed from my armpits when I was 15 due to bad add-vice I was convinced was a good idea. It changed the way my body is able to regulate my body temperature and left me with big scars I was equally insecure about for a long time. I still get pit stains because sweating is how the body detoxes, which I didn't fully understand back then when I thought a slice and dice would fix my insecurities, but I've helped save others the pain and shame of following in my footsteps because I dare to share my experience; yet another example of 'that is what you should not do, now let that be a lesson to you' but had he denied me my wish I would have felt less empowered to choose for myself and others may have harmed themselves because my testimony wouldn't have been able to dissuade them from it so it wasn't all for nothing. Cutting out irregular or dysfunctional parts without dealing with the underlying energetic cause only creates issues elsewhere later and is part of the cultural shift we must make now.

He helped me switch schools in grade 10 when I was tired of feeling like I didn't matter at the first high school I attended which may have been a perception but the switch brought together tribes that may not have otherwise got together and families were created from that.

He drove me to the airport when I was 16 and flew to Saint Boniface, Winnipeg for my first EXPLORE bursary that I discovered

I was eligible for in the guidance counsellor's office at Holy Trinity Catholic High School where I finished my secondary schooling.

He drove me to the train station for my second EXPLORE bursary in La Pocatière, Quebec when I was attending McMaster University and was granted the opportunity again.

He even took me to Toronto to audition for Canadian Idol two mornings in a row because I wanted to try out and he was willing to help without complaint. Both mornings I remember waking up to Michael Bublé's song 'Home' but didn't take the hint. I'm glad how it worked out.

He was consistently there for me and gave me a job each summer in harvest until school started and he found a replacement. That was a blessing I took for granted but appreciate now!

I cry tears of gratitude for all the big things he helped me do and all the small things too.

He was the one who put his foot down when I didn't believe I had what it took to complete University given the trajectory an early relationship would have set me up for and today I have an English degree because I respected his perspective enough to shift gears and get recommitted in a different program for which I am grateful.

My Dad has been a pillar of strength throughout my life and in 2019 when I faced a lot of my own shadow I drained him energetically when pulling out of the city gig destroyed my INNER WEB and I felt lost because I couldn't get this book done either. And then months later when I publicly outed patterns that directly impacted our family and then blamed him for not helping me get out of a mess I'd got myself into, I devastated him without consideration. I am not proud of how I acted.

Through the con video game I got FEARFULL and judgemental that he couldn't see what I've laid out here with greater clarity than I had in the beginning but I didn't have the picture put together quite as well as I thought I did and compassion was definitely missing when my joker archetype was active in its scared side.

The joker archetype in its scared side is the shadow side of the trickster which often emerges to experience, express and expose dysfunctional social norms and unpopular issues not generally spoken of in polite society. My family were hurt by the repressions I was ruthless in outing as I let this archetype lead me to disobey social rules, etiquette and conventional behavior without consideration for those I love and who'd always been there for me, to which I can only say I'm sorry, please forgive me, I love you, thank you for everything and I promise to do better now that I know myself better.

Sacred Contracts says the joker or trickster archetype in its sacred side "can be a great ally in presenting you with alternatives to the straight and narrow path, to people and institutions who seek to hem you in through peer pressure and conformism" as we've seen in the con exposed here with more consideration for loved ones and fellow players of the game.

I have not been an easy daughter to love, as most crazy and strong-willed ones aren't, but he has been the best Dad I could possibly have asked for. And so I make the end of this story about one half of my beginnings because he deserves that much and so much more.

Earlier this year my heart started to thaw out and I stopped trying to push my BS onto him or others because I saw how ineffective that approach was proving to be and I realized just how much I needed to rebuild the bridges I'd burned with the one man, other than my Papa, who's always loved me even though I've put him through so much.

The night I had to call for help because I'd got the underbelly of my car caught up on a huge block of ice at the end of a treacherous washout zone that had refroze and thawed with the changing temperatures earlier this year, without my being informed or aware, I saw the symbolism of my own need to soften my frozen heart.

Dad and Bonnie showed up when I called after driving around the country block thinking I'd be right at the start of the flooded area like a normal person but instead I'd hit the slushy ice path going so fast I just kept going and had got to the very end before I couldn't make it out on my own. Dad and Bonnie pushed while I reversed, having kicked out a bunch of the ice and slush before they got there, and once I broke free from the block I was hung up on he got in and backed my fabulous Fiesta out of troubled waters for me. Bonnie and

I talked and hugged for the first time in two years and the healing began.

Miraculously I didn't destroy the bottom of my car and the night after that crazy episode while driving home from helping a friend I heard Old Dominion's song "One Man Band" play on the radio which I hadn't heard since when Goom was in hospital. I remember dancing to it on repeat for months, wishing for the man I look forward to sharing my life with (less the trashing hotel rooms or getting tattoos piece); it was the first time I'd heard that song play on the radio since then so I felt like Goom was riding with me. When Cody Johnson's "Til You Can't" played next, I drove past the dark house I was in alone while Papa was in hospital recovering from a fractured pelvis and went to make amends with the greatest man I'm glad I came through. It was a start and dropping the heart walls hurt feelings lead me to put up is what we must all do as we settle our differences and choose love where loss was rewarded before.

I feel like we've been brainwashed to think our 'virtual families' matter more than the people we were born to who may not understand what we're trying to do, especially during these divisive times, but the ones who love us to the limits of where they can and wish only the best for us are worth doing better for; if you've got a Dad (or Mom) like I do then it's time we do our best to heal the hurts that FEAR caused both parties and stop letting our BS divide us.

Not doing so means giving the slow and steady divisive strategy of the evil being employed against us now the upper hand and that is not the kind of band I want to be playing with when the curtains come down and we feel a clown because we lost sight of what matters.

At the end of the day our people are who we'll turn to when we're in trouble, or have cause to celebrate, if we haven't pushed them away by trying to sell FEAR in a different way. Competing beliefs culturally make us feel like we're living in disconnected realities and there is truth to that because belief systems are vibrational because they are charged by emotions just as the Highrise of Emotional Awareness portrays. Disconnected BS results in cognitive dissonance and an insightful video on YouTube about this is by 'Academy of Ideas:

Free Minds for a Free Society' called "MASS PSYCHOSIS – How an Entire Population Becomes MENTALLY ILL." The concept of mass psychosis was debunked by fact checkers who referenced a particular academic whose recent research projects seem to have been funded by sources with conflicting interests. For the sake of not calling certain individuals out I'll not use any names but simply say it's a great example of why discernment of information and sources of it based on interests and alliances matters in a world with a biased public domain.

No one can jump through a screen to help if they don't know where we are so let's build back better starting at home, where we live our daily lives, and connect the dots through compassionate connection in common unity without trying to impose our BS on one another.

Bringing PEACE to the world only works if we have it within us to bring forth so let us dare to do the INNER work that helps love win.

We are the players on the field of life who are all co-creating the realities we believe to be true, as per the allegory of the cave. May we support ourselves and one another in facing the shadows that scare us so that we can true-lie bring the sacred back to the throne we lead our lives from without causing harm, loss or fraud to our fellow man.

Laura JeH - Namaste (the light in me honours the light in you)

Useful Books Referenced & Recommended

Allen, James, 1864-1912. *As a Man Thinketh*. Peter Pauper Press, 1951.

Brown, Brené. *Gifts of Imperfection: Let Go of Who You Think You're Supposed To Be and Embrace Who You Are*, Hazelden Publishing, 2010.

Cholmondeley, Zorah. *The Enchanted Garden: Conscious Gardening with the Fae and Nature's Elementals*. Clairview Books, 2021.

DeRohan, Ceanne. *Right Use of Will: Healing and Evolving the Emotional Body*. Four Winds Publications, 1986.

Estés, Clarissa Pinkola. *Women Who Run with the Wolves : Myths and Stories of the Wild Woman Archetype*. Ballantine Books, 1992.

Ford, Debbie. *The Dark Side of the Light Chasers: Reclaiming Your Power, Creativity, Brilliance, and Dreams*. Hodder & Stoughton, 2001

Glasser, William. *Warning: Psychiatry Can Be Hazardous To Your Mental Health*. Harper-Collins Publishers, 2003.

Godin, Seth. *What to Do When It's Your Turn (and It's Always Your Turn)*. Do You Zoom, Inc., 2014.

Hay, Louise L. *You Can Heal Your Life*. Hay House, Inc, 1999.

+ audioprogram by Napoleon Hill referenced called: *Outwitting the Devil*

Lipton, Bruce H. *The Honeymoon Effect: The Science of Creating Heaven on Earth.* Hay House, Inc, 2013.

Maltz, Maxwell. *Psycho-Cybernetics: A New Way to Get More Living Out of Life.* Wilshire Book, 1976.

Melchizedek, Drunvalo. *Living in the Heart: How to Enter into the Sacred Space Within the Heart.* Light Technology Pub, 2003.

Myss, Caroline. *The Anatomy of the Spirit: The Seven Stages of Power and Healing.* Random House, 1996.

Myss, Caroline. *Sacred Contracts.* Random House US, 2013.

Ruiz, Don Miguel. *The Four Agreements: A Toltec Wisdom Guide.* Amber-Allen Publishing, 2001.

Shinn, Florence S. *The Game of Life and How to Play It.* DeVorss, 1925.

+ audioprogram by Florence Scovel Shinn referenced called: *The Magic Path of Intuition*

Williamson, Marianne. *A Return to Love.* HarperCollins, 1996.
* The poem *Our Deepest Fear* can be found here with permission to use granted*

Printed in the United States
by Baker & Taylor Publisher Services